DYNAMO AND VIRGIN RECONSIDERED

Essays in the Dynamism

of Western Culture

The MIT Press
Massachusetts Institute of Technology
Cambridge, Massachusetts, and London, England

DYNAMO AND VIRGIN RECONSIDERED

Essays in the Dynamism

of Western Culture

LYNN WHITE, JR.

Set in Linofilm Baskerville by Argee Incorporated.
Printed and bound in the United States of America
by The Colonial Press Inc.

Originally published as *Machina ex Deo*

First MIT Press paperback edition, June 1971
Second printing, March 1973

ISBN 0 262 23032 1 (hardcover)
ISBN 0 262 73024 3 (paperback)

Library of Congress catalog card number: 69–10843

To My Children

The cultural patterns which are emerging to-day are largely a result of the impact of technology and science upon the traditional Hellenic and Christian assumptions of the West. Since both our scientific and our technological movements are in great part products of these same Greek and Semitic legacies as they fused and took shape in medieval Europe, we are involved in a feedback process of great historical intricacy.

Those of us who spend our lives scrutinizing the past in order to grasp the present are suspicious of all-inclusive interpretations of human destiny. It is our habit to study any large problem the way we look at a statue: by walking around it. Sometimes we come close to inspect a detail; then we stand back for more perspective. From various stances it looks very different, but the contradictions are not necessarily incongruous, since each view is partial. I have tried to see our new culture from several angles of vision which are deliberately chosen because they are appropriate to some aspect of the subject.

The collecting and revising of these essays was occasioned by the very diverse reactions to a study of ecology in *Science* for March 10, 1967, which here appears as Chapter 5. As I watched the sparks fly, I realized that both the enthusiasm and the rage which the study evoked were caused by the fact that it was written in the context of a larger pattern of thinking which has not occurred to most people. Ansel Adams, whose photographic lens has enabled him to probe deep into the relation of man to nature, wrote to me, "You have summed up a number of basic and opposing forces of which 'conservation' (as we know it) is merely a 'surface effect.'"

This small volume is an effort to analyze the nature of those forces and the changes which they are bringing about. The first chapter describes what a historian can do to clarify such matters. The second deals with what has happened to the Hellenic tradition among us; the third (in a very different mood because the problems have another tonality), with the Christian. Chapters 4 through 10 deal largely with engineering and, to a less extent, with science, exploring some of their roots and fruits. Chapter 11 is a coda pondering the fearful psychological perils inherent in rapid cultural change. I shall succeed in my purpose if these pages lead some readers to look at themselves and our world with fresh eyes.

Lynn White, jr.
Department of History
University of California
Los Angeles

The author is indebted to the publishers or editors of the following journals and books for their permission to reprint material in this volume in revised form: Chapter 1, *The Journal of Higher Education* (October 1961); Chapter 2, Harper & Row, Publishers, Incorporated, *Frontiers of Knowledge in the Study of Man,* copyright 1956; Chapter 3 *The Journal of the History of Ideas* (April 1942) and Rutgers University Press, *Ideas in Cultural Perspective* (1962); Chapters 4 and 8, *The American Scholar* (Spring 1958 and Spring 1966); Chapter 5, *Science,* copyright March 10, 1967 by the American Association for the Advancement of Science; Chapter 6, the Center for the Study of Democratic Institutions, *Science and Democratic Government,* ed. C. F. Stover (1963), and *Science, Scientists and Politics* (1963); Chapter 7, *Technology and Culture* (Fall 1962), published by the University of Chicago Press; Chapters 8 and 9, *Engineering, Its Role and Function in Human Society,* ed. W. H. Davenport and D. Rosenthal, copyright 1967 by Pergamon Press, Inc.; Chapter 9, *The Journal of Engineering Education* (January 1967); Chapter 11, *The Saturday Review* (November 1954).

CONTENTS

THEN AND NOW

1

In our American culture, "social responsibility" is, by axiom, a good thing. Anybody not claiming to be endowed with it is obviously socially irresponsible and therefore abetting the forces of disintegration. In this matter, nuances are considered to be evasions. As a nation we like to operate with dualisms rather than pluralisms, two-party systems rather than political spectra. We are suspicious of spectators who can enjoy a game without yelling loudly for one side.

This is not a view of reality or of morality in terms of which most professional historians can work comfortably. Historians are inevitably citizens and taxpayers; they are generally parents; not infrequently they have been soldiers. As persons they are "engaged," profoundly involved, in concrete social responsibilities. But as historians they know something of the history of history, and they are not happy about past efforts of historians to exercise social responsibility through their profession.

For generations German historians have been dedicated to overcoming the political splintering of Germany which resulted from the medieval battle between Papacy and Holy Roman Empire. To the west they saw France, Britain, and Spain—even little Holland and Portugal—building powerful colonial empires, whereas Germany, like Italy, wallowed in a morass of political confusion which was the heritage of centuries of factional strife. They dreamed of the great days of the Ottos, the Henrys, the Fredericks, and longed to restore a Germanic Empire which once more should awe Europe by its might. The greatest series of historical texts ever published, the *Monumenta Germaniae Historica,* was edited by a passionate group of superb scholars who, after the shake-up of the Napoleonic Wars, felt that Germans might be unified by becoming newly aware of their medieval glories. Their organization, formed in 1819, took as its motto *"Sanctus amor patriae dat animum."* When Bismarck inaugurated the Hohenzollern Empire a half-century later, the *Monumenta* was its intellectual cornerstone.

The German historians of the nineteenth century were explicit and vastly successful in the exercise of what they regarded as social responsibility. Nor did they see any conflict between their ethics as historians and their obligations as citizens. But we can now perceive that they were building not only a united Germany but a Germany united in authoritarian terms. The tradition of German historical thinking is today so permeated with statist values that many liberal Germans are in despair. A thoughtful West German scholar once said to me, "I am convinced that we shall not be able to build a really democratic Germany until the formal study of history is abolished at every level of German education."

He added, "You Americans are fortunate. Because the first great stratum of your national glory is involved in a democratic Revolution,

your study of history in the schools is biased in
the liberal direction." Could they have heard this remark, most Americans would have turned to the nearest American historian with warm congratulations. But the historian himself, in proportion to his personal commitment to the democratic ideal, would resent the implication that history is by its nature propaganda for or against some structure of social values. He would feel that the German scholar who made the remark, and who considered himself a democrat, was in fact showing the totalitarian taint in its most subtle and pernicious form.

The historian, when he is awarded his Ph.D., takes no Hippocratic oath that he will permit nothing to divert him from searching for ascertainable truth about the past. Yet members of his guild in democratic nations are as deeply committed to the ideal of objectivity as are physicists. They are passionately convinced not only that their professional ethics is in harmony with the democratic concept but that the deliberate manipulation of the past for present ends, however good, undermines democracy by puppetizing the citizens' minds.

Disconcertingly few laymen — even few college graduates — really understand what the scholar means by "truth." It is not a citadel of certainty to be defended against error: it is a shady spot where one eats lunch before tramping on. The professional thinker enjoys being where he is, but he also looks forward to new vistas around the next bend, over the next crest. Traditionally, most people have thought of truth as something "known," absolutely. In reaction, many have now swung to the opposite form of absolutism: the agnostic assurance that nothing is either known or knowable, that all truth is no more than a matter of taste. In the historical trade, this kind of polarization between absolutes is known as "dogma eat dogma": great sport as spectacle but intellectually profitless.

The daily, most intimate experience of the historian in his own research denies both of these concepts of truth. History does not exist; all that exists is debris—scattered, mutilated, very fragmentary—left by vanished ages. Each historian knows that by his own labors in scrutiny of the rubbish heaps, he arrives at more and more understanding of what happened in the past. The historian believes that such understanding is worth his life, for two reasons.

First, understanding is the highest human function. We abdicate our humanity, and perhaps our hope of divinity, in proportion as we decline to be interested in anything as material to be understood and mastered. Modern scholarship's mood cannot be grasped without remembering its clerical origins. On ceremonial occasions the professor wears his truest garments, a priest's cassock and biretta and a monastic hood, all inherited from his professional ancestors, the faculties of the medieval universities. Most of the luncheon chitchat in a faculty club is deceptive; it conceals a profound emotional commitment, a "calling," a vocation in the religious sense. Some cynicism about clerics has always been justified, and it is equally warranted about academics. But if one lives in the university world, one knows that some are called to be entomologists, and others to be etymologists, and others to be historians. Each is "led" irrationally to dedicate his reason to the understanding of some class of phenomena. Each, likewise, has a priestly sense of responsibility to convey to others the grace of his accumulating insights.

Second, and more specifically, the professional historian believes that his particular discipline has a peculiarly important spiritual function (although most historians would recoil from expressing it so). Human nature is the most complex phenomenon which we know. The core of its complexity is the puzzle that a man should wish to understand not only his natural environment but also himself. Historians generally agree with Socrates that the chief purpose of life is to "know yourself." History is the attempt to understand human nature in all its varied capabilities and limitations through the study of all that we can know about what people have done and thought and felt.

One hears, these days, much deploring of academic ivory towers. No professional thinker will repudiate the symbol, even though he may question the material; quite the contrary, he will insist that part of his job is, for certain purposes, to extricate himself from all immediate practical concerns, from all contemporary value

6 judgments. In climbing his tower he does not necessarily repudiate these concerns or judgments; it is simply an essential, although intermittent, part of his methodology—like a monk's fasting—which is designed to give new kinds of vision. From the somewhat abstracted top of the tower he can sometimes see things not so easily perceived from the bottom. A virologist may fear cancer and suspect that there is often some relation between virus and the start of malignancy, yet he knows that too exclusive a concern with this possible relationship may well cause him to overlook aspects of virus which may, in the long run, illuminate any such relationship, and which are worth understanding quite apart from any connection with cancer. Similarly, a historian is convinced that he handicaps his research if he is too constantly trying to come up with useful findings.

Even the most self-consciously antiquarian historians, however, cannot evade the fact that their results are, in the mass, very useful indeed. A scholar of my acquaintance who, at the slightest suggestion that he has utility, pounds the table and cries, "I speak only *dead* languages!" is in fact contributing greatly (as he well knows but declines to admit lest he please Philistines) to our knowledge of the vast cultural osmosis which, through thousands of years, has gone on between East Asia and the West: a mutual debt that must be recognized and appreciated by both sides if the present tensions between Asia and ourselves are ever to be harmonized in a stable emotional context.

Since each of us, and all the world's societies, have sprung from the past, memory is inevitable. But how accurate is folk memory, natural recollection of things vanished? One need not be a Freudian to recognize that pride, selfishness, and trauma warp and distort the memories not only of individuals but also of groups. Often a muddied memory generates a dangerous phobia or sets up a block to reasoned action. In psychoanalysis, the analyst, realizing that he will never know all of his patient's past, nevertheless hopes to filter out the repressed elements sufficiently to clarify the murky parts of it, so that the patient can act rationally, having been released from his past.

Similarly, the historian lays humanity on the couch. Aware that he knows very little of the past, nevertheless he knows enough to illuminate many dark closets of our group memories and to exorcise the ghosts that paralyze men into inaction or frighten them into ill-considered action. After a century, the United States, both Northern and Southern, is still hagridden and immobilized in many areas of its national life by the memory of the Civil War and Reconstruction. Yet such works of critical scholarship as Vann Woodward's *Strange Career of Jim Crow* have helped the slow progress of unshackling us from our past. Again, North Americans react with surprised self-pity when faced with the deep hostility toward us which is found in Latin America, even in circles which, we feel, should appreciate our consistent nobility. We shall not be able to act or react sensibly in relation to that vast region until as a people we have reviewed as accurately as we can the history of our relation with the Southern nations since the Alamo. Reciprocally, many of the sins which our neighbors lay to the *yanqui* might appear to them to have quite different origins if Latin Americans themselves made a greater effort at objectivity in recalling their own checkered past. Only by such group psychotherapy can we free ourselves from folk memory in order to act discerningly and vigorously in terms of present actualities.

Most historians would insist that we cannot "learn from history" in the vernacular sense of the phrase. History has no predictive value. Of itself it can provide us with no plans of action appropriate to any new situation. Historians conceptualize remains from the past into patterns of interpretation. But these intelligible schemes never seem to them to be exactly, or even approximately, repeated. In each new situation, as they see it, the variables are at least as significant as the constants.

For this reason, Arnold Toynbee, despite his great general reputation, has little standing among professional historians—and not from envy or myopia. The specialists who have the most detailed knowledge of the individual cultures of the past simply do not find adequate evidence to support Toynbee's insistence upon repetitive features in the record.

For this reason, likewise, the practice of building theoretical models, a fashion that is currently sweeping economics, sociology, political science, and even anthropology, stirs little enthusiasm among historians save as a fascinat-ing intellectual phenomenon, the history of which must someday be written. If a model embraces two sets of events, it must disregard the unique elements in each. As the model expands in scope, it is necessarily removed further and further from more and more of the actualities in concrete situations. Such constructs often have great elegance, but their beauty may be both intellectually and practically perilous if it leads us to forget the factual data which necessarily were discarded as the model emerged. Like Ulysses, the historian binds himself to the mast of the ascertainable facts, both repetitive and unique, lest the siren song of models draw him overboard into a sea of too arbitrarily achieved theory.

Now

The historian's method, of course, likewise demands selectivity among the available facts. But it is a different sort of selectivity, based on the assumption that the key to understanding a complex human situation is as likely to be found in the unique and novel detail as in a trait common to somewhat similar situations.

History is worth knowing, historians believe, because the past happened, and our race is possessed by a spiritual necessity to try to understand all that was or is. As for the future and the molding of it, most historians have an equal conviction about the study of history. From the kaleidoscopic and iridescent record of mankind, we can learn chiefly this: the possible range of human thought, emotion,

10 organization, and action is almost infinite. In facing today's problems, we must therefore liberate ourselves from presuppositions as to what may or may not be possible. Knowledge of history frees us to be contemporary.

Although inevitably we are the offspring of the past, we are mutants as well. We are living in a time of general shift more fundamental than any since agriculture and herding displaced food-gathering and hunting as the habit of human existence. Not only the outer forms of living are being remodeled: our standards of values, thought, and conduct, our criteria of judgment, all of our yardsticks are altering as well. The very canons of our culture are changing.

What are these changes of canon?

For one thing, ever since the days of the Greeks our thinking has been framed within the *canon of the Occident.* This is the unexamined assumption that civilization par excellence is that of the Western tradition; that history is essentially the stream of events which began with the siege of Troy and which gradually expanded from its first drama in the Levant to find ever wider stages in the Mediterranean of the Pax Romana, the Europe of medieval Latin Christendom, and the North Atlantic civilization of so-called Modern Times. All else—the epic spectacles of Peru and Mexico, of Islam, India and further India, of China, Korea, and Japan, even of that extraordinary Eastern Christendom of Byzantium and Russia —was either irrelevant or at best a cabinet of curiosities. To us, Man has really meant European-American Man: the rest were "natives."

12 We may snicker at the California country pastor who habitually prayed "for the conversion of the heathen in the heart of Africa where the foot of man has never trod," but his naïvete illustrates what we are outgrowing. Our image of the person is ceasing to assume tacitly that the white man is made peculiarly in the likeness of God.

The canon of the Occident has been displaced by the *canon of the globe*. Today everything from Communism to Coca-Cola is becoming worldwide in its range. This has the ring of platitude only because we have accepted it so completely in the realm of international politics. Few of us realize the extent to which our most ordinary actions and thoughts are today being formed according to non-Occidental models. Admitting that we are change-prone, just why do we change as we do? There are superficial reasons indeed, but no really adequate explanations for such casual facts as that the use of vodka, for example, is growing very rapidly in America today, or that in any large liquor store one can buy saki, a beverage practically unknown among us a few years ago. Of making cookbooks there is no end; but why, suddenly, is there a market for innumerable ordinary kitchen-shelf cookbooks which, without cultural pretensions or hands-across-the-sea flourishes, simply assimilate the skewers of Armenia, the woks of China, and much else to everyday American cookery?

To be sure, no great culture of the Old World has ever been entirely isolated: borrowings have been constant. The eighteenth century loved *chinoiserie* and took to drinking tea out of porcelain cups—equipped, we may note, with un-Oriental saucers into which one might pour the tea if it were too hot. But this was consciously a fad; we today are different in the extent of our readiness to assimilate alien influences and our relative unconsciousness about the process. For several decades China and Korea have been the chief factors in furniture design from Los Angeles to Stockholm. A bride, recoiling from her mother's taste, today chooses the new without thinking of its Asian inspiration, which in any case is largely masked by the cliché of "functionalism." And Japan is the obvious source of most that is best in contemporary American and European domestic architecture. Not long ago a group of American ladies arranged to entertain some visiting Japanese students with a house tour of the finest recently built homes in their community. The students remained in a state of courteous boredom—after all, all this looked pretty much like grandmother's house on Kyushu—until they burst into arm-waving enthusiasm over the sparkling gingerbread of an immaculately preserved Victorian villa which their hostesses had added to the tour to show how we had progressed. Clearly, while the Western tourist wails that the Orient is being "ruined" by Occidental influences, the Oriental may rightly feel that from his standpoint the West too is losing its distinctive and "picturesque" qualities by overmuch orientalization.

"But," objects the diminished ghost of Plato, "tacos and pilaff, crockery and bedposts, are not the essence of a civilization: it is *ideas* that are really important. Quite naturally our Asian friends have been taking over the superb philosophical concepts which are in the public domain of the West, but can it be shown that we are absorbing anything equivalent from them?"

For the moment, but only for the moment, let us refrain from looking at the structure of values which underlies the question; it can perhaps be answered in its own terms.

For far more than a century, since the days of Schopenhauer and Emerson at least, the professional thinkers of the North Atlantic civilization have been consciously subject to Asian influences, but these have been regarded as an exotic rather than an integral element in our thought. In the last two or three decades, however, the psychoanalytic movement, the study of semantics, and the intricate skein of philosophies and theologies labeled Existentialism have combined to challenge the ancient Platonic-Cartesian dualism which polarized experience between mind and body, spirit and substance, time and eternity, man and nature, natural and supernatural. Because of all this we are at the moment peculiarly vulnerable to influences drawn from the stream of Buddhist thought which rose first in India and flowed in a broadening current through China to Japan, where it came to be known as Zen. With an almost unbelievable sophistication, but naturally in terms of their own tradition, the Zen thinkers

faced and pondered many of the issues which
are uppermost in the minds of the Western linguists, psychologists, and philosophers to-day; and these latter, whether directly or by reflection, are finding light from the East. Prophecy is rash, but it may well be that the publication of D. T. Suzuki's first *Essays in Zen Buddhism* in 1927 will seem in future genera-tions as great an intellectual event as William of Moerbeke's Latin translations of Aristotle in the thirteenth century or Marsiglio Ficino's of Plato in the fifteenth. But in Suzuki's case the shell of the Occident has been broken through. More than we dream, we are now governed by the new canon of the globe.

One reason for the subtly pervasive influence of Zen among us, even upon those who have never heard of it, is its challenge to a second major canon which we inherited from the Greeks: *the canon of logic and language.* For more than two thousand years in the West it has been axiomatic that logic and language are perfected instruments of intellectual analysis and expression. The training of our minds has consisted essentially of getting skills in logic, whether in its philosophical or its mathematical form, and in language, by which we have meant the European and, until recently, the classical tongues. Much of our present discussion of ed-ucation is still based on the premise that the mind which has mastered logic and language is able to achieve clear and efficient results in any field.

But there is a new and more complex canon

today, one which does not deny the validity of the canon of logic and language but which puts it into a wider context, just as the canon of the globe does not negate the canon of the Occident but changes it nature by amplifying it.

This second new canon is the *canon of symbols.* It insists that logic and language are neither perfected nor infallible, but rather that they are simply two most marvelous, and still evolving, human devices closely related to a cluster of similar inventions of symbolic intellectual instruments: the visual arts, literature, music, dance, theater, liturgy, mythology, formulations of scientific law, philosophical patterns, and theological systems. A symbol may be a novel, a creed, a formula, a gesture, or a cadence, as well as an image, a word, or a crescent, cross, or swastika. We are beginning to see that the distinctive thing about the human species is that we are symbol-making animals, *Homo signifex,* and that without this function we could never have become *sapiens.*

For we have not only a capacity for making symbols; we are under necessity to create them in order to cope humanly with our experience. An orangutan or a tiny child may manage in terms of things immediately sensed or remembered as sensed. But thought or communication involving relationships or generalizations, much less any complex imagination of what might be compared with what is, seems to demand symbols. For practical purposes we do not and cannot deal with things in themselves; we must deal with signs pointing toward things.

The fact that these signs are arbitrary to the point of whimsicality is not a defect but a virtue; each arbitrary creation may open new vistas to the mind's eye. If this book were in Hopi, it would still convey much the same ideas, but some probably a bit more lucidly and some a bit more obscurely, for each convention of symbols has its peculiar capacities and weaknesses. Our race needs both Hopi and English.

The mathematicians above all others have discovered the utility of developing different symbolic grammars which may be mutually contradictory but which are functional so long as they are internally coherent. In 1733, as intellectual sport the Jesuit Girolamo Saccheri challenged Euclid's axiom of parallels, and substituting the "nonsensical" axiom that through a given point two lines may be drawn parallel to a given line, he constructed a self-consistent non-Euclidean geometry. Unfortunately, he laughed it off as a *jeu d'esprit*. Not until four generations later did mathematicians realize that he had made a great discovery. Then a whole constellation of contrasting geometries burst forth, and it was with the light of Riemannian geometry that Einstein found the mathematical key for the release of atomic energy. The most astonishing part of the new canon of symbols is the discovery that we human beings can deal with facts only in terms of fantasies. We have begun to understand the instrumental validity of arbitrary symbols.

Indeed, even the way our senses report experience to us may be structured by the conventions of language, art, or the like. An American psychologist studied changes in perception and methods of solving problems which took place among members of the Baganda tribe in Uganda as they learned English and came under European influence. He gave them pieces of cardboard of different shapes, sizes, and colors and asked them to separate them into piles. Those who had been in English-language schools almost always divided them according to color, as Westerners do. Those who had had few European contacts built piles on the basis of size or shape, but almost never according to color: the language of the Bagandas is almost entirely lacking in words for colors, and evidently the tribesmen are simply not equipped to detect such variations. If Homeric Greek makes no distinction between blue and green, can we be sure those less blind than Homer were able to see the difference? And when, toward the middle of the thirteenth century, Villard de Honnecourt appends to his sketch of a lion the proud scribble "Note well that this lion was drawn from life," should we be astonished that his lion is exactly one of those tame little poodle-lions, with a mane of symmetrical ringlets, universally found in late Romanesque and early Gothic sculpture? In every society there is a convention of vision, and perhaps of each of the senses.

A most important aspect of the canon of symbols, therefore, is our realization that while symbols are created by us, these creatures in a peculiar way come alive, turn upon us, and coerce us and our experience to conform to their anatomy.

For example, any man who makes it his business to observe American women closely will quickly discover that in our land women are emotionally dependent on men in a way quite different from that in which men are dependent on women. Despite all the proud talk of sex equality, women themselves refer to "hen parties" with contempt and to "stag parties" with a twinge of envy. The reasons for this widespread and unwarranted feminine sense of being secondary are many, but at least one of them is linguistic. The grammar of English dictates that when a referent is either of indeterminate sex or of both sexes, it shall be considered masculine. The penetration of this habit of language into the minds of little girls as they grow up to be women is more profound than most people, including most women, have recognized; for it implies that personality is really a male attribute and that women are a human subspecies. It is dramatized in the old story of the suffragette struggle in Britain, when a young recruit to the feminist forces burst into tears after a little clash with police over picketing. "My daughter, don't despair," said a seasoned campaigner. "Pray to God and She will give you strength!" It would be a miracle if a girl baby, learning to use the symbols of our tongue, could escape some unverbalized wound to her self-respect, whereas a boy baby's ego is bolstered by the pattern of our language.

Intuitions of this sort, related to the new canon of symbols, lead us on to the recognition of a third major change in the canons of our culture. From the Greeks again, we inherit the *canon of rationality*, which assumes that reason is the supreme human attribute and that anything other than rationality is "less" than rationality and to be deplored as subhuman. It assumes that disagreements are not fundamental, and that with adequate reasonable discussion and examination of the evidence, a single truth will emerge acceptable to all men.

But now we dwell in a world dominated by the *canon of the unconscious.* Closer scrutiny of our mental processes has shown that a vast lot is happening in the shadowy iridescence, the black opal of the abyss which lies within each of us. Our scientists in particular have become fascinated by the problem of the genesis of original ideas, and have resuscitated the word "serendipity" to label one of the most curious aspects of intellectual creation: the seemingly instantaneous discovery of something entirely unexpected in the course of hard work toward a different goal. The word was invented in 1754 by Horace Walpole from the Oriental legend of the Princess of Serendip: she had three suitors, to each of whom she assigned an impossible task; all three failed, but in the course of his heroic struggles each accomplished something even more marvelous. Every scholar and artist has in some measure experienced serendipity: the sudden welling up into consciousness of insights, intellectual structures, visions which clearly would never have come had the conscious mind not been in travail, but of whose gestation we had no forewarning. Reason is not all of the mind.

For many centuries such thinkers as St. Thomas Aquinas, so rationalist that they perceived some limitations of reason, groped toward a picture of the human mind as a shiny sheet of metal, part of which is bent back upon itself so that it is mirrored in itself. Reason is the part of the mind which is capable of reflection—that is, of contemplating its own processes. The rest of the mind perhaps does not differ from reason in its essential qualities, particularly in creativity. But unfortunately we cannot yet easily watch it in action.

As the chemistry and physiology of our nervous system become clearer, experimental means of peering into these mysteries may be developed. To date, the psychoanalytic assault on the problem of the unconscious has been the most sustained and probably the most rewarding. Yet its very success has opened up new complexities: the unconscious seems to be as deeply conditioned by cultural forms as is the conscious mind. Surely the relative scarcity in America of the Oedipus complex, at least in its "classic" Freudian form, is related to the contrast between the paternal monarchy of the nineteenth-century Viennese family and the chaotic town-meeting government of the typical American family of recent decades.

The social psychologists, anthropologists, and historians are proving helpful in this exploration of the unconscious. For example, it is becoming clear that episodes such as the slaughter of the Jews by the Nazis, or the more recent resurgence of witchcraft and witch hunting in Africa, are intelligible not in terms of the functioning of the rational faculty but as group responses to spiritual crises, as means of coping with and "explaining" deep psychic disturbances produced by catastrophic shifts in the cultural foundations. The linguists analyzing non-European tongues have reached similar insights: language structures, social relationships, and cosmologies often have a related pattern among a given people, and the emotions and unconscious attitudes as well as the verbalized ideas of participants in a culture seem to be shaped by these as definitely as a Flathead Indian's brain is shaped by the headboard of his papoose cradle.

The human mind is not completely conditioned. It can achieve an extraordinary degree of freedom and "objectivity." But we have come to see that logical reasoning and rational confrontation of relevant evidence are only part of the task if true freedom is to be won. The idea that there are unconscious areas of the mind is not new, but in no previous era, of Western thought at least, has it loomed so large or challenged us so insistently. The realization of the scope, the dangers, and the potentialities of the unconscious is essential to our new image of the person.

It is significant that more and more we are using the word "unconscious" rather than "sub-

conscious." The latter is involved in meta-
phorical association of up-and-down spatial relationships with value judgments, and it thus
might trick us into assuming that the unconscious is in some way *sub* and therefore inferior
or unworthy. This aspect of the new canon of
the unconscious illustrates the fourth, and final,
major change of canon which is observable in
our culture.

Although some of the earlier Ionian philosophers seem to have had a different bent of
mind, ever since the great days of Athens we
have generally thought, felt, and acted in terms
of the *canon of the hierarchy of values.* We
have assumed and consciously taught that some
types of human activity are more worthy of
study and reverence than others because the
contemplation of them seemed to bring greater
spiritual rewards. This hierarchy of values, expressed most clearly in the ancient concept of
the liberal arts, was codified in the Middle
Ages, expanded in the Renaissance and post-
Renaissance, and has continued to be manifest
in emphasis on the importance of mathematics,
logic, philosophy, literature, and the unapplied
sciences. Within its self-imposed limitations,
this tradition of personal cultivation and of
education had an unsurpassed richness and
intellectual magnificence.

But large parts of human experience and
creativity were omitted from the upper rungs
of this ladder of values which provided the pattern and rationale of our inherited culture.
Anything, above all, which required the use of

the hands was excluded, not only rigorously but with some indignation, from the area of prestige which was reflected in the older liberal arts curricula. It was shut out because the top brackets of culture and education were the perquisite of an aristocracy which used not its hands but its brains. The Greeks and Romans, living in a slave economy, considered use of the hands banausic and contemptible. Primitive Christianity, largely a proletarian movement, had contrary instincts which were perpetuated by the medieval monks and by their Protestant ascetic offshoot, the Puritans. But the notion that work with the hands is integral to the good life was slow to make an impression on our cultural tradition, presumably because society remained largely aristocratic or hierarchical in organization. Today we have forgotten, or can scarcely believe, the degree to which manual operations were once avoided by those who were, or aspired to be, of the upper crust.

The secret of the almost explosive originality of our times is the wiping out (save in certain cultural backwaters) of the ancient barrier between the aristocrat and the worker. Americans, whose ancestors first created a large-scale equalitarian community, should take particular pride in this reunion of the human hand and brain into their proper organic whole: the ideal image of the person is no longer the armless *Venus of Melos*. Yet even in America our language and our presuppositions are still so permeated by the inherited aristocratic tradition that it is hard to put into words just what is

involved in the fact that the combined democratic and technological revolutions have made
both workers of us all and aristocrats of us all;
that the two sets of values, historically so sharply
divided, are now confused and must be schematized according to a new plan.

This plan is emerging: the old canon of the
hierarchy or ladder of values has turned at
right angles to become a new *canon of the
spectrum of values.* Whereas the old canon insisted that some human activities are by their
nature more intellectually and spiritually profit-
able than others, the new canon holds that
every human activity, whether changing dia-
pers or reading Spinoza, whether plowing for
barley or measuring galaxies, enshrines the
possibility—perhaps not the actuality but the
potentiality—of greatness: its proper contemplation and practice promise the reward of insight. "What is the Buddha?" asked the Zen
novice. "Three pounds of rice," replied the
abbot.

"All the road to heaven is heaven," said St.
Teresa of Avila. The notion of a spectrum of
values, as distinct from a hierarchy of values,
challenges all the dualisms which, among us
Occidentals, for over two thousand years have
divided the seamless coat of actual human experience. The path and the goal, means and
ends, becoming and being, process and purpose
—all these fuse into nowness. We are no longer
under compulsion to violate immediacy: each
perception, whatever its nature, may be the
beatific vision, each moment orchestrated for

Gabriel's trumpet. Just as the economic and political revolutions of our time have produced an egalitarian society, so our intellectual revolution has insisted on—what would have seemed a logical and semantic absurdity to former ages —an equality of values. Indeed, we suddenly realize the weakness of our verbal symbols: clearly "value" is a monetary metaphor, inherently scaled up and down rather than sideways. Yet we have no other serviceable word, so we must use the term "value," understanding in what sense it is obsolete.

Just as aristocratic forebodings that a democratic social order would necessarily mean the end of personal cultivation and individualism have not been realized, so democratic insistence on the equal potential worth of what have been called "values" does not inevitably lead to mental or emotional drabness. On the contrary, it can open our eyes to the spiritual possibilities inherent in types of experience and creativity which, because of a divided society and class-centered education, could not be envisaged as a whole by any previous generation.

It compels us, for example, to redefine our notion of "genius" to embrace kinds of originality hitherto overlooked. Sometime about 1420 an unknown carpenter or shipwright, presumably a Fleming, invented the bit-and-brace, thus making possible continuous rotary motion in boring. By that act he invented the compound crank and precipitated the greatest single revolution in the design of machinery; by 1430 we find machines involving double

compound cranks and two connecting rods. No
unconscious "evolution" led to the brace; it was created by a leap of the mind which imagined and implemented a new kinetic pattern which has been fundamental to the development of modern society. Until we have learned to look at the carpenter's brace with a certain awe, we have not begun to absorb the cultural implications of the democratic revolution.

All four of the old canons which have suffered a sea change in the storms of our time were formulated by the first consciously Occidental society, that of Athens. In the realm of thought and emotion, twenty-four centuries of Hellenic dominance now are ended. The marvel is not that our vision is confused but rather that we are learning so quickly how to view mankind from vantage points other than the Acropolis.

Whenever there is major change there is likewise risk of great loss. If this analysis of the four mutations of canon which are going on around us is correct, what are the cultural treasures which may be endangered by this flux?

Does the change from the canon of the Occident to the canon of the globe in any way diminish the wonder, the amazing variety and spontaneity of the Western tradition in which we Americans stand? No; but it imposes upon us the difficult problem of how to become citizens of the world without uprooting ourselves from our native soil. A superficial cosmopolitanism is no adequate substitute for a cultural parochialism which makes up in spiritual depth what it lacks in breadth. How are we to become cultivated in global terms when most of us don't manage it in Occidental terms?

The canon of logic and language has become the canon of symbols. Are logic and language less important than formerly? No; now we can envisage and use them as parts of a vastly expanded set of tools of analysis and communication. But whereas once a person could confidently regard himself as educated if he were competent with these two instruments (including, of course, mathematics), how is each of us today to learn to handle the rest with facility, or even to know what is happening when other people are employing them? In a brief life which can accommodate only a short period of formal education, how can we learn the vocabulary, grammar, and semantics of drama, dance, music, and the like? How can we explore the mutually contradictory but often coherent thought structures of the major philosophers, and learn to use them, as a mathematician uses the different incompatible geometries, each to achieve a variant quality of vision? How can we find time or imagination enough to encompass the language of myth? How can we come to understand, from the inside, why Newton considered himself almost more a theologian than a mathematician? The peril is that, like small children suddenly taken to a new land with a strange speech, we may become tongue-tied. Indeed, the state of much current literature, music, and art makes one fear that this is in fact happening.

Now that the canon of rationality has become the canon of the unconscious, does this mean that we should simply assume that we and all other people are essentially irrational and need no longer bother with the disciplines of reason? No; it means that we have come to realize more clearly than ever before the psychological, biological, and cultural context of the rational function. We have recognized the chances that self-interest or self-deception will mask itself quite honestly as rationality. That we name such cover-up thinking with the popular word "rationalizing" shows how deeply this conception has penetrated the general mind. We have put our idea of the conscious mind into the frame which in fact it has always had, and ‧by this sharper delimitation of its bounds we can become more aware of the nature, the uses, and the glory of rationality. Yet, when all this is said, to many temperaments the canon of the unconscious is an invitation to let the reason become lazy.

Finally, since revolution has swept aristocracy into the cracks and corners, does the shift from the canon of the hierarchy of values to the canon of the spectrum of values mean that the values cultivated by the aristocracies of the past are obsolete? No; on the contrary, if we neglect them we are betraying the democratic revolution which was an effort to upgrade the masses and not to downgrade them. Yet in the long perspective of human history our revolution is so new that we do not really know what a high democratic culture would look like, much less what its formal education—that is, its organized plan for cultural transmission—would be. The task of understanding ourselves and the world we live in is vastly complicated by the democratic necessity of supplementing the well-formulated aristocratic values with others, more nebulous at present because never adequately verbalized, which for millennia have been held by the common people to be equally necessary and worthy of respect. In general these latter values have centered not, like those of the aristocrats, in government, religion, and art, but in the home, the daily relations of people in the community, and the skills of production and craftsmanship. The task is not simply to add these to the traditionally cherished values of the upper classes, but rather to smelt all human values down and to recast them as a unit. Until this is done we shall continue in a state of cultural confusion; but the blast furnace is only now beginning to glow hot.

Each of these four basic changes of canon is a green apple in the bad case of intellectual, social, artistic, and moral dyspepsia from which we are all suffering at present: there is more to be digested than our bellies can handle. There are some, of course, who think that they can vomit the substance of the modern world and nourish themselves on savors wafted from the past. But most of us will say with Adelard of Bath, eight centuries ago, "I'm not the sort of fellow who can be fed with the picture of a beefsteak!"

Only one aid to digestion appears. Practically every book we read, every speech we hear, every TV show or moving picture we see, every conversation around us, is formulated and phrased, at least on the surface, in terms of the four old Greek canons of the Occident, of logic and language, of rationality, and of the hierarchy of values. This outer form, however, is a violation of the inner substance. In theological terms, our culture has experienced transubstantiation, and it is our spiritual task to recognize the actualities and not be deceived by the accidents. It would be useful as an intellectual discipline to apply to our analysis of what goes on about us the four new canons of the globe, of symbols, of the unconscious, and of the spectrum of values. Since each of them is no more than a cultural reflection of a changed concept of what a human being is, these canons may help us to understand not only our age but also ourselves.

As we saw in the last chapter, for more than two thousand years Greek patterns of thinking were fundamental in our culture. Today they are being vastly expanded and changed; but this is only part of the intellectual and emotional upheaval of our time.

From the fourth century until the middle of the seventeenth, and even, although with decreasing vigor, until the middle of the nineteenth, the astonishing Jewish heresy called Christianity was the chief force shaping the new superstructures which the European and American mind built on the Greek base. Whether by its direct action or by reaction against it, whether through its doctrinal formulations or through the secularized vestiges of dogma which became the liberal creed of the Enlightenment, the Church proved herself, when not the *mater,* at least the *matrix,* of Western thought.

Yet during the past three centuries, and especially the past three generations, Christianity has been shaken not so much by external attack as by internal crisis. The Church and its cargo weathered not only the tempest of the barbarian invasions and the collapse of Antiquity, but likewise survived without irreparable damage the much less difficult squalls marking what is generally considered to be the passage from the Middle Ages to modern times.

Now, however, a greater peril has appeared; what the storms have spared, the worms may be destroying. The timbers of the Ark may no longer be sound.

This religious crisis lies at the very vortex of the maelstrom of our time: to maintain the contrary is to misunderstand the place which Christianity occupied among us for fourteen centuries, and which, in some part, it still holds. Yet while contending floods of polemic literature have swirled about the discoveries of Copernicus, Darwin, and the biblical critics, not enough attention has been given to the exact and sympathetic analysis of the difficulties besetting traditional theology. Perhaps the issues have been too palpitating to encourage objective examination: agnostics, inflamed with an almost evangelical zeal, have been bent on smashing ecclesiastical "infamy" with every available bludgeon, while theologians have fought a rear-guard action, chiefly, it would seem, with intellectual smoke screens designed to cover retreat. But surely we cannot understand the fevers of our age until we arrive at the true historical diagnosis of the malady afflicting contemporary religion; and for this a preliminary dissection of the anatomy of orthodoxy is indispensable.

The Christian claims to be unlike other men: he dwells amphibiously in two worlds. Born into the realm of time, he is likewise sacramentally *renatus in aeternum.* As a result, for the Christian every event has a double but unified significance appropriate to the duality of his experience. He enjoys two modes of perception, two distinct but simultaneous ways of viewing each phenomenon; he has two types of information, not *drawn* from time and eternity respectively, but *seen* from them just as we see a thing through two eyes. He likewise uses two methods of expressing these parallel perceptions: one is history; the other is myth.

History is a coherent account of events which occurred in time. Speculation about the general nature of the time sequence is therefore an inevitable by-product of the writing of history, and more remotely, of the effort to make ethical decisions for action. Greco-Roman antiquity held to various notions of cyclical recurrence, usually involving degeneration within each cycle, or less frequently, to a theory of endless and meaningless undulation. Faith that the historical process is unique and that it has a moral purpose first appeared in Europe as a Christian dogma, the elements of which were mainly taken over from popular Judaism. The Hebrews seem to have started with the usual Mediterranean legend of the Golden Age of innocence, the Garden of Eden, and to have thought of history as a progressive decay, through Adam's fault, possibly in cycles. The Jewish people, however, were intense patriots, and under Assyrian, Babylonian, Persian, and Macedonian conquest they never lost hope that someday Jehovah would make Israel, his chosen race, supreme over the whole earth. They came to feel, under the religious leadership of the Prophets, that they were a nation with a moral mission in history: to set up God's kingdom on earth and to teach the gentiles his will. But successive uprisings and defeats convinced many Jews that only supernatural aid could accomplish this end, aid in the form of a Messiah. Mingled with these Messianic hopes there flowed a turbid stream of apocalyptic thought, springing (it would seem) chiefly from Persian sources, and teaching a Last Judgment over which the Messiah should preside at the end of historical time.

Inevitably, it was in terms of some such view of the nature of history that the preaching of Jesus was understood by his first followers. And when his life and words were, in their eyes, completely validated by what they believed to be his resurrection and ascension, they naturally felt that what had been in a sense hypothesis was now proved fact: "Since by man came death, by man came also the resurrection of the dead." Adam's fall explained the coming of the Messiah, and Jesus' death and resurrection pointed clearly toward his return and judgment. Consequently, the Christian view of history carried a power of immediate and overwhelming conviction: it was no longer mere speculation, but rather it was based on the empirical fact of a historic personality. The significance of that fact, however, was understood in terms of Adam's fall and the expectation of the judgment; to Christians this symmetrical interpretation of history came to be as important as the fact of Jesus because it made the Incarnation intelligible.

Naturally, to the early Christians, the pagan belief in purposeless temporal undulation was entirely unacceptable, and the idea of cosmic repetitive cycles was the worst of blasphemies. From such a theory it follows, writes Origen, that "Adam and Eve will do once more exactly what they have already done; the same deluge will be repeated; the same Moses will bring the same six-hundred thousand people out of Egypt; Judas will again betray his Lord; and Paul a second time will hold the coats of those who stone Stephen." Obviously no such notion could be held by a Christian. "God forbid," cries St. Augustine, "that we should believe this. For Christ died once for our sins, and, rising again, dies no more." The axiom of the uniqueness of the Incarnation required a belief that history is a straight-line sequence guided by God. And as the Church became the exclusive cult of the Roman Empire, the doctrines of undulation and recurrent cycles vanished from the Mediterranean world. No more radical revolution has ever taken place in the world outlook of a large area. In the early fifth century St. Augustine elaborated on Judeo-Christian foundations the first developmental philosophy embracing all human history. During the Middle Ages and Renaissance, step by step, this Augustinian providential interpretation was very gradually secularized into the modern idea of progress, which until recently dominated Western historical thinking.

But today an increasing group of historians, disenchanted with historical optimism, confess that the idea of human progress is intelligible only in terms of the theological assumptions on which it originally rested: without the dogma of the Incarnation, the dynamic and recti-linear view of time traditional in our Western culture (a concept which has done much to invigorate that culture) tends to die out. Having lost faith that God revealed himself uniquely at one single point in history, we are relapsing, they say, into the essentially static or repetitive view of the time-process typical of Antiquity and of the East. It is increasingly evident that history as Westerners generally have conceived it is an expression of Christian ideas about the nature of time.

The second means of expressing Christian experience is myth, defined as the dramatiza-tion in temporal terms of things seen from the nontemporal standpoint of eternity. The Church salvaged from pagan mysticism a mode of thinking which permitted the abstraction from temporal happenings of universals which seem to manifest themselves repetitively in time; and myths were developed as the best means of sharing the perception of these uni-versals. Despite its fictional form, myth is not mere fiction. A myth is not about something that once happened, but rather about some-thing that is always happening: the narration of an eternal event. Myths are firmly anchored to the world of everyday happenings because they dramatize the universals which have been thought to be discoverable behind temporal events, However, unlike the historian, the myth-maker starts not with the particular, but, by illumination of the spirit, with the abstraction of something timeless. The experiential basis of myth-making can perhaps be grasped, at least by analogy, from Mozart's supposed letter to a friend:

The whole composition, though it be long, arrives in my head almost complete, so that I can survey it, like a lovely picture or a beautiful person, at a glance. In my imagination I do not hear the parts successively, but I hear them, as it were, all at once . . . . And to hear them thus, all together, is much the best way!

Similarly, some fourteen centuries earlier the Neoplatonist Sallustius remarked of myth that it "did not happen at any one time, but always is so: the mind sees the whole process at once; words tell part first, part second."

Myth-making is therefore an analytical process, with an element of arbitrary art in it. Myth is successful to the extent that its dramatic sequence enables any one meditating on the myth to reverse the analysis, to synthesize and to share the eternal perception from which the myth-maker started. It is a legitimate and necessary form of symbolic expression, closely akin to allegory, to dramatic poetry, and to fable. But although one may discuss a myth, one can never completely convey or explain its content in any other medium, because in the best myths dramatic presentation still leaves many meanings compounded in a counterpoint of significance which is destroyed by further analysis. Even when myth is believed to be identical with history, it is always enveloped in an atmosphere of *double entendre,* and, as though to insist that it never really happened in time, it incorporates elements of wonder and fantasy.

For example, consider the very simple myth, told in the valleys of California, of how the orange got its golden color. A long time ago the fruit of the orange tree was a dingy brown, like a potato. But when Herod commanded the slaughter of the children of Bethlehem, St. Joseph and St. Mary fled with the baby Jesus to Egypt. After days of journeying across barren mountains and hot desert they at last reached the great valley, green against the desolation, and sank down exhausted in an orchard of oranges. And the trees in compassion bent their branches low, offering their fruit to the Holy Family. Seeing which, the Christ Child smiled and blessed the trees; and ever since then the fruit of the orange has been like gold of the Mother Lode.

Clearly the eternal event dramatized in this myth could not be expressed so compactly in any other way. Merely to assert that a Christ-like person glorifies all nature, to say that the creature is redeemed by love of its Creator, that man is saved by sacrifice, is only to scratch the surface of the verities which through mythical form are perceived "all together," fused in simultaneous harmony.

Myth-making is found not simply among primitive people but among civilized as well; no sharp line can be drawn between Homer and Aesop. However, it is true that while the myths of primitive cultures deal frankly with the gods and achieve their antihistorical emphasis by

means of miracle, the myths of advanced societies, in which a more vivid sense of the transcendence of the divine has been achieved, generally try to express eternal events by other
means, replacing miracle by deliberate and
sometimes comic unreality. But whether it be
simple or sophisticated, myth attempts for eternity what a prism does for light; it breaks up
various elements which are found unified and
entire, and presents them in sequence to the
human eye.

Since ideologically the Christian moves in two
planes at once (time and eternity, nature and
grace), he sees everything as both history and
myth. To be sure, the historical content of Christian myth-history has at times been tenuous in
the extreme. The Virgin Birth, for example,
quite apart from difficulties arising from its ad-
mittedly miraculous character, would appear to
be denied by the very documents upon which
it purports to rest, inasmuch as the genealo-
gies preserved in the Gospels of St. Matthew
and St. Luke both trace the descent of Jesus
from King David through St. Joseph and thus
flatly contradict the Nativity stories contained
in those same records. But the Virgin Mother,
undefiled yet productive, bearing Christ into
the world by the action of the Spirit of God, is
so perfect an analogue of the most intimate experience of the soul that powerful myth has sustained dubious history, for to the believer, myth
and history have been one.

The traditional Christian world view is bifocal. Inevitably, therefore, paradox is the most

natural style of Christian formulation. Beliefs which to the logical secular mind (limited as it is to the temporal perspective) seem mutually exclusive are to the Christian mutually sustaining. To adopt another, and perhaps more exact, metaphor from physics, the Christian life is conducted in the magnetic field between the poles of time and eternity. To destroy either pole would destroy the magnetic field, the vital tension which keeps the Christian life healthy; and that is what the Church has commonly meant by heresy.

This bipolarity between myth and history, eternity and time permeates all Christian institutions and doctrines, although the relative importance of the two elements has varied greatly in different periods. The chronic tension in Christendom between the priestly and the prophetic traditions is generally represented as a conflict between conservative and radical, but it goes much deeper; it reflects the clash of two types of religion, the active and the contemplative. The one, primarily Jewish in origin, emphasizes conduct and the bringing in of the Kingdom of God on earth; the other, Greco-Oriental, is chiefly concerned with the salvation of the individual, conceived as a member of a timeless *civitas Dei*. No sooner had the Edict of Milan in 313 made Christianity a tolerated religion than this struggle came into the open and rocked the Church. In 314, at the Council of Arles, it was decided that the validity of a sacrament does not depend upon the morality of the priest officiating. Since that day Christianity has tended to fluctuate between puritanical moralism and amoral sacramentalism. Fortunately, despite wide variations of emphasis between different centuries and different groups, the great body of Christians has kept the middle ground of orthodoxy, has balanced its perceptions of time against those of eternity, and, in disregard of all logic, has successfully combined in its doctrine of the Church the mutually exclusive conceptions, on one hand, of the dynamic, visible *ecclesia militans,* a "saving institution" trying to draw men to God, and, on the other hand, of the contemplative, invisible *ecclesia trimphans,* "the body of the elect," enjoying, whether in this life or the next, the beatific vision.

In specific matters of dogma the bipolarity of time and eternity, history and myth is so evident that illustrations may be chosen almost at random. The Roman Catholic Church has long discouraged discussion of the logically insoluble problem of free will versus predestination; and in 1937, assembled at Edinburgh, the leading theologians of the Protestant and Eastern Churches similarly affirmed both contradictory doctrines, declaring that no attempt to reconcile them philosophically can be considered part of the Christian faith. Seen through the bifocal glasses of Christian experience there is, indeed, no conflict: God in eternity has predestined every action, but we experience our temporal destiny as freedom. To a philosopher this does not make sense. But that does not disturb a Christian, who claims to know things of which philosophers are ignorant. The same may be said of the dogma of the human and divine natures of Christ, declared at Chalcedon to be perfect, each in its own way, not identical and not separate. Temporally and historically, Jesus is, according to the creeds, completely human. Eternally and mythically, Christ is God. No one has ever pretended to tell what this means, but millions have claimed it to be the central fact of their experience. Similarly, the Kingdom of God is eternally "within you" and temporally "to come." And nowhere is the paradox made necessary by Christian bifocalism more evident than in the contradictory doctrines of the Judgment. Immediately at death there is a preliminary judgment, since through death the soul passes out of the category of time. But at the end of historical time all the dead will rise for a final judgment, which logically is superfluous. Clearly, however, these two judgments are the same supposed phenomenon viewed first eternally and then temporally.

To summarize: the Church has never doubted that God exists outside the categories of space and time. God made time as a function of his creation; but in God there is neither before nor after: in the words of the Johannine Christ, "Before Abraham was, I am." Time is a human mode of perception; it does not limit God. Everything that has ever taken place in time, or will take place, existed (and exists) in God's mind, or, to speak in temporal terms, in God's foreknowledge and intention, before the Spirit brooded over the waters. And this includes the

Fall of Adam, the Incarnation of Christ, the
Last Judgment, and the detailed history of
every individual soul.

As a result, the Christian lives in a peculiar
state of consciousness, mixing inextricably the
temporal and the eternal. The keenest intellect among theologians, St. Thomas Aquinas,
coined a word to express it: *aevum,* as distinct
from *tempus* and *aeternitas.* He defines *aevum*
as "the mean between eternity and time," *medium inter aeternitatem et tempus,* partaking of both.

The Christian, then, aspires to dwell in both
time and eternity. He insists with all his might
that God works in history, but he knows likewise that in the pilgrimage of his own soul the
whole historical drama of salvation is recapitu-
lated, and, as in the Negro spiritual, he trembles
at the mystery of it: "Were you there when they
crucified my Lord?" Transcendent reality re-
veals itself historically to the race and in parallel
myth to the individual. Adam fell, and falls in
us; God became man but once, yet the Christ
child nestles next to every heart touched by the
Holy Spirit; a young man once hung on a cross
in perfect and complete atonement for the sins
of all generations, yet he bleeds on every altar;
Christ rose, and we rise in Christ; he will come
again, and he comes perpetually; he will judge,
and we are daily judged.

This belief in a double manifestation of the
divine mind through identical history and myth
has been the very core of Christianity, enabling
men to conceive in time, and thereby to become, what eternity is.

But by the end of the last century this bifocal Christian world view had been rendered untenable in the thinking of countless millions. The Copernican revolution was slow to undermine it, probably because the new cosmology, which in no way challenged the concept of a creation, seemed at first to have little relevance to time and history. However, as men came to believe that every star was a sun, and that surely, in the depths of space, there must be other inhabited worlds, each with its own history and therefore with sin and the need of redemption, doubts arose: in the newly discovered universe one Bethlehem seemed scarcely sufficient. The Church saw the peril from afar, and sent to the stake Giordano Bruno, the first great evangelist of "the infinity of worlds." For, as the Fathers had so vigorously asserted, to a Christian time must be unique: there cannot have been two historic Incarnations. The notion of the plurality of inhabited spheres seemed to challenge the Christian axiom that the drama of sin and salvation is played but once.

Attempts were made to assimilate the new astronomy to the Catholic tradition, but too often these degenerated into fantasy. For example, in the *Traité de l'Infini Créé,* widely circulated in the later eighteenth century, the anonymous author, probably a cleric, posits in the infinite universe an infinity of Saviors supervising an infinity of Last Judgments, and ingeniously suggests that when each planetary system is dissolved at its Judgment, the saved are mustered to form a legion of angels, led by their particular Man-God, to battle for redemp-

tion of souls in less complete worlds, whereas
the damned become demons with contrary intent. Such extravagances helped to discredit the notion of a plurality of *Heilsgeschichten,* but could not altogether obscure the objections which modern astronomers had raised to the inherited Christian view of the time process. The effort to encompass the new cosmos within the great tradition culminated, in the last year of Victoria's reign, in Alice Meynell's *Christ in the Universe:*

With this ambiguous earth
His dealings have been told us.   These abide:
The signal to a maid, the human birth,
The lesson, and the young Man crucified.

But not a star of all
The innumerable host of stars has heard
How he administered this terrestrial ball.
Our race have kept their Lord's entrusted word.

Of his earth-visiting feet
None knows the secret, cherished, perilous,
The terrible, shamefast, frightened, whispered, sweet,
Heart-shattering secret of his way with us.

No planet knows that this
Our wayside planet, carrying land and wave,
Love and life multiplied, and pain and bliss,
Bears, as chief treasure, one forsaken grave.

Nor, in our little day,
May his devices with the heavens be guessed,
His pilgrimage to thread the Milky Way
Or his bestowals there be manifest.

But in the enternities,
Doubtless we shall compare together, hear
A million alien Gospels, in what guise
He trod the Pleiades, the Lyre, the Bear.

O, be prepared, my soul!
To read the inconceivable, to scan
The million forms of God those stars unroll
When, in our turn, we show to them a Man.

Yet with all its sincerity and insight, this poem
marks a fateful break from orthodoxy: the
uniqueness of time and history is gone: Christ
is become Krishna of the myriad Incarnations.

And already the revolution in biology had
given the *coup de grâce* to the traditional Christian interpretation of history. Hitherto Christian myth and Christian history had been the
same; Adam falls when we sin (that is the myth),
but in fact Adam did fall (that is history); by
sacramental grace we rise from the dead in
Christ (that is the myth), but all of Christian
history pivots on the dated resurrection of a
historical man, Jesus of Nazareth; Christ judges
us in our every act (that is the myth), but Christ
may come on clouds of glory tomorrow morn-
ing (that has been the historical expectation of
the Christian community). Christianity above
all other religions had rashly insisted that its
myth really happened in time. It was not merely a dramatization of the common denominator
of all religious experience: it was likewise a sequence of historic events. But the traditional
Christian history has depended for its validity
upon its symmetry: it must stand or fall as a
unit. If historically one man, Adam, did not fall,
then the unique historical Incarnation of God
in one man, Christ, loses its point, and the expectation of the historical Last Judgment crum-
bles. But by the later nineteenth century most

educated men had concluded that as a temporal fact Adam did not fall. Doubtless theories of evolution would continue to be modified, but no conceivable mutation of biological science could rehabilitate Adam as a historical individual.

The new astronomy had undermined confidence in the uniqueness of the Incarnation; the new biology destroyed the symmetry of Christian history which had been designed by the devout to explain that Incarnation. Consequently, in the opinion of many men, the entire structure collapsed, and faith in the singleness and purpose of the time process waned. Under the aging Victoria, there occurred a shift in the world outlook of Europe and America more important than any since the days of Constantine. If the latter marked the beginning of the Middle Ages, historians of the future, gifted with a perspective denied us today, may well conclude that the former marks their true end.

For multitudes reared in the traditional faith, the bipolarity which had been basic in Christianity seemed now lost: the pole of eternity remained, but the pole of time had been destroyed, and with it vanished the magnetic field in which, for nearly two millennia, the Christian life had flourished. To many intelligent men and women whose hearts yearned to be Christian, this crisis marked the end of Christianity; if the nexus of myth with historical fact was broken, then, they maintained, the myth loses its conviction. Or, as others have suggested, the

American and European mind is so steeped in respect for concrete fact that it instinctively rejects the myth or symbol which strays too far from history. If this diagnosis be correct, then we seem doomed to succumb to one of the new and dynamic myth-making religions which now for decades have been waging their *jihads:* to some successor of National Socialism, with its consciously formulated myth of the chosen race making history under a Messianic leader; to Communism with its new Israel, the proletariat; or more probably, to some fanaticism not yet envisaged. Our political maladies are integrally related to our religious uncertainties. Myth-history Western men must have; and if Christian myth-history fails them, they will find it elsewhere.

But to sing a Requiem for Christianity may be premature. Now for decades some of the keenest theologians have been hailing the smashing of the traditional myth-history as pure gain. Merely as a conspicuous example: Reinhold Niebuhr, the most seminal religious thinker of America, stoutly maintains that myth is the necessary language of religion, but that no myth is capable of conveying its full freight of truth until it is a "broken" myth—that is, one which is severed from history and clearly recognized to be a sign pointing from the temporal order to a reality beyond. "What is true in the Christian religion," he writes, "can be expressed only in symbols which contain a certain degree of provisional and superficial deception." Even about Jesus we must tell little lies in the interest of a greater truth: "The message of the Son of God who dies upon the cross, of a God who transcends history and is yet in history, who condemns and judges sin and yet suffers with and for the sinner, this message is the truth about life. It cannot be stated without deceptions but the truths which seek to avoid the deceptions are immeasurably less profound. Compared with this Christ who died for men's sins upon the cross, Jesus, the good man who tells all men to be good, is more solidly historical. But he is the bearer of no more than a pale truism."

Here indeed is something new in Christian theology! Rejecting the old identification of myth and history, it is an effort to validate the significance of history by transcending the temporal facts of history. To compare the Jesus of history unfavorably with the Christ of myth, to go on to speak disparagingly of "the chronological illusion" in regard to the Last Judgment, this is to make a virtue of the catastrophe which has destroyed the traditional Christian bifocalism.

But many who are drawn toward such views accept them reluctantly, fearing lest indifference to history bring some diminution of ethical fervor: the Christian myth, they agree, remains "true," but the stripping of the historical husk from traditional dogma would seem to deprive the time process of moral meaning. When faith in the righteous culmination of history is lost, men look for the vindication of their ideals outside history. When time is conceived to be vagrant, morality is cultivated as an ascetic means of reaching spiritual perfection and of transcending the senseless flux. In such a religious atmosphere the belief emerges that while the individual man may be moral, society is immoral by its very nature, since it is hopelessly enmeshed in a temporal tangle having no reference to eternal reality. Personal ethics may survive, but the activist, the prophet, and the champion of social justice go unheeded because men of religion have lost interest in history: temporal events are an illusion, a veil through which sage and saint try by meditation and worship to penetrate toward the timeless Absolute. To many Christians, social ethics has significance, prophetic religion has a dynamic, only in the framework of that purposive view of history which Christianity inherited from the Jews and which now would appear to have been destroyed.

We may, indeed, be turning in the direction of the Orient. In the East, especially in India, men have never taken history and time very seriously or felt them vividly to be real. Buddhism and Hinduism, in particular, have consciously elaborated and used myths as symbols of eternal truths quite without concern for historical accuracy. By losing its focus on time and history, by concentration on eternity and myth, Christianity might, in fact, be able to influence the Orient more easily than has proved possible with its traditional historical-activist emphasis. But would we Westerners, trained so long by Christianity itself to think in historical terms, have any truck with an eternity-oriented cult?

Clearly, of all types of Western Christianity, Roman Catholicism, which concentrates its devotion upon the timeless Bethlehem and Calvary of the Mass, can most easily adjust itself to the new religious tendencies. Indeed the papal promulgations in 1854 of the dogma of the Immaculate Conception of St. Mary by St. Anne, and in 1950 of the dogma of the bodily Assumption of the Virgin into heaven, show that the average Roman Catholic, unlike the average Protestant, is already able to find complete religious satisfaction in myth which has no relation to documented history. But for two centuries the various Protestant Churches, led by the Methodists and Anglicans, have almost instinctively been adapting themselves in a Roman Catholic direction. The Orientals, who have long claimed that our Occidental activism is a symptom of religious immaturity, may therefore be complacent at the prospect that out of the present religious crisis, the greatest since that of Antiquity from which Christianity itself emerged, there may well come a more quietistic and contemplative form of Western religion.

Our later twentieth century is, in fact, more hospitable to the idea of a religion expressing itself in terms of arbitrarily constructed symbols than would have been conceivable even fifty years ago. Contemporary psychology, philosophy, semantics, linguistics, mathematics, and aesthetics are permeated by the recognition of the necessity of symbolic systems not merely for communication but for thought, and to some extent even for sensory perception itself. Today not merely all myths but all other symbols as well are "broken"—that is, they are seen to be not descriptions of things symbolized but signposts pointing in the direction of things. Yet without such arbitrary symbols we cannot cope with experience; we can know fact only in terms of fancy. Even in dealing with the beliefs of "primitive" peoples, scholars no longer use the word *superstition* with its old self-assured ring. Indeed it is a word which has gone out of style, not through indifference to error but because we see that error is inherent in all observation of fact.

In such a context, does the breaking of Christian myth-history have the shattering consequences which once it seemed to have? Adam indeed is gone, but sin remains; the apple is withered, but the moral perils of new knowledge have never been more evident; the serpent crawls away, but not temptation. The eternal event, the thing which "always is so" is unaffected by changes in cosmology or biology. Christian myth remains the most compelling expression of man's timeless spiritual experience evolved by any religion.

As the dust of old scientific-theological controversies settles, one thing grows clearer: like the first disciples, we still stand facing a cross, a love, and an agony which demand explanation. Drawing on its Jewish traditions, the early Church flanked the cross with an apple at one end of time and a trumpet at the other. That symmetry is destroyed, but its crux remains. In every age men have cast a net of symbols to catch truth, and it is the nature of symbols that as their mesh is fine they obscure what they capture. Yet in each generation this man who was crucified reaches through the enveloping web and touches us with bleeding hands; and we may touch his side.

The Education of Henry Adams is a classic in the proper sense that, while it is read by few, it has helped to shape the notions and emotions of millions of Americans who have never even heard of it. Adams, both a grandson and a great-grandson of Presidents of the United States, was thwarted in his own political ambitions and so turned his devious and subtle mind to the problem of the dynamics of human destiny. In his old age he became less a historian than a philosopher of history. "I don't give a damn what happened," he exclaimed to a friend. "What I want to know is why it happened."

But he was a historian-philosopher with the soul of an artist even though, by his own wry diagnosis, being "a quintessence of Boston . . . [his] instinct was blighted from babyhood." As an artist he groped for symbols—not only words but images.

His first great image came to him in the summer of 1895 when, with Senator and Mrs. Henry Cabot Lodge, he toured Normandy and the neighboring regions: Amiens, Bayeux, Coutances, Mont-Saint-Michel, Vitré, Le Mans, Chartres. He had, of course, known of the things he saw; but now, suddenly, he grasped them. Or rather, these incredible churches of the twelfth and thirteenth centuries seized him and shook him until his intellectual teeth rattled. What force had impelled men to infuse stone with such striving and restlessness, and to fling it high into heaven? Why had they filled acres of windows with throbbing colors such as a Yankee had never dreamed of? Why had they enriched every portal and pinnacle with figures from earth, hell, and paradise?

All of these buildings were shrines of St. Mary the Virgin, the Mother of God. It was she, the Queen of Heaven, who had commanded and inspired this titanic outburst of cultural vitality. To explain to himself and to America "why it happened," Henry Adams wrote *Mont-Saint-Michel and Chartres,* a work of genius but very personal in its interpretation. For Adams' Virgin is not what medieval Catholicism had thought its Virgin was: she is, rather, the life force, the wellspring of fecundity, "reproduction—the greatest and most mysterious of all energies." She had been the Oriental fertility goddesses, Diana of the Ephesians, Venus. In her Christian garb, however, whether "symbol or energy, the Virgin had acted as the greatest force the Western world had ever felt, and had drawn man's activities to herself more strongly than any other power, natural or supernatural, had ever done."

But Henry Adams was puzzled as to why this force, formerly so irresistible, had declined. "The Woman had once been supreme; in France she still seemed potent, not merely as a sentiment, but as a force. Why was she unknown in America? . . . American art, like American language and education, was as far as possible sexless. Society regarded this victory over sex

as its greatest triumph." Clearly, America was
bowing down before some new power. What
was it?

In 1900, at the Trocadero Exposition in
Paris, Adams found his second image, the dynamo. "Among the thousand symbols of ultimate energy, the dynamo . . . was the most ex-
pressive." To him it became "a symbol of infinity." He felt it to be "a moral force, much as
the early Christians felt the Cross." A profound
change had taken place in the nature of civilization: "The new American, like the new European, was the servant of the powerhouse, as the
European of the twelfth century was the servant of the Church."

Although it was written in 1905, *The Education* was not published until 1918. It was ini-
tially read by an America emerging from the
First World War, vastly puzzled by its new global power and recoiling from the responsibilities
which are the reverse side of power. Having
lately become the world's greatest industrial
complex, the United States pictured itself as a
country youth just arrived in the big city. It romanticized its agrarian past and the supposed
simplicities and warm virtues of an age that had
vanished. The Bureau of the Census announced
that the frontier had closed in 1890, and Henry
Adams proclaimed 1900 as the end of the era
of the Virgin and the beginning of the reign of
the dynamo. The contrast between his symbols
fitted the mood of the nation.

But Adams' images have continued to fasci-
nate thoughtful people because they embody

the deepest intellectual issue of our century. Three hundred years ago "modern" philosophy was born when Descartes separated the realm of mind from the realm of matter more sharply than had ever been done before in history. The attributes of matter were mass, extension, and motion, all of which can be handled mathematically. Colors, textures, sounds, and eventually all the most vividly human experiences and values were declared to be essentially "subjective," and in some way "unreal." Even in the eighteenth century it was being remarked that "Descartes has slain poetry." Physics and chemistry made immense strides; by the late nineteenth century their industrial applications were spectacular; and at last, despite the Romantic reaction, scientist and engineer seemed to dominate the Atlantic civilization. What eluded the mathematical method came to be thought of as illusion, or at least as some strange accident unrelated to the nature of things. People forgot (what St. Augustine had known) that the very concept of number, not to mention the higher reaches of mathematics, was an artifact of, if not a revelation to, the human mind, which cannot be understood in terms of nature devoid of mind. As the nineteenth century gave way to the twentieth, all that was most human —goodness and beauty, love and sacrifice— seemed most exiled from the "real." In 1903 the young Bertrand Russell gave ultimate expression to the tragedy which is implicit in the Cartesian separation of mind from matter:

That Man is the product of causes which had no prevision of the end they were achieving; that his origin, his growth, his hopes and fears, his loves and his beliefs, are but the outcome of accidental collocations of atoms; that no fire, no heroism, no intensity of thought and feeling, can preserve an individual life beyond the grave; that all the labors of the ages, all the devotion, all the inspiration, all the noonday brightness of human genius, are destined to extinction in the vast death of the solar system, and that the whole temple of Man's achievement must inevitably be buried beneath the debris of a universe in ruins—all these things, if not quite beyond dispute, are yet so nearly certain, that no philosophy which rejects them can hope to stand. Only within the scaffolding of these truths, only on the firm foundation of unyielding despair, can the soul's habitation henceforth be safely built.

Henry Adams, too, was an orthodox Cartesian, dedicated to salvaging the human values of history by the discovery of laws analogous to those of physics: "a historical formula that should satisfy the conditions of the stellar universe." His most fantastic effort in this direction was an essay, written in 1908, on "The Rule of Phase Applied to History," in which, following a mathematical hypothesis set forth by Yale's Willard Gibbs, he proposed that social transformations are comparable with the phases of matter seen in the change of a solid to a liquid, or of a liquid to a gas. To him the Virgin and the dynamo represented two successive and radically contrasting phases of human destiny.

And yet these two great symbols, designed to achieve intelligibility for the human condition, only served to underscore human defeat. *The Education of Henry Adams* is one of the most reticent of autobiographies: emotion is many layers below the surface. But at his death, in a wallet of very special papers, a lyrical and agonized

62 "Prayer to the Virgin of Chartres" was found which incorporates a prayer to the dynamo clearly prophesying—in 1906 at the latest—the destruction of humanity by atomic energy. The Virgin represented all that was distinctively human, all that the Cartesians regarded as "subjective"; the dynamo pointed to the annihilation of all human values, first by the achievement of an antlike society, and then by the victory of impersonal cosmic force over all life.

This is the dread of the twentieth century. Admitting that we have many totalitarianisms and may have more, admitting that the atom is a peril, nevertheless are we justified in believing with Henry Adams that human values are engaged in a last and hopeless duel not only with the death wish in our own natures but with the entropy of the universe as well? Symbols are not merely means of expressing thought about experience; often they impel us to schematize our understanding of experience in their own terms. Are the dynamo and the Virgin in fact opposing and mutually exclusive energies?

Even Adams saw the joke when, in the summer of 1904, he bought a French automobile in which to go on pilgrimage to the shrines of Our Lady. However dissimilar spiritual and mechanical forces might seem, the student of history was able to fuse them happily for professional purposes. Was this just a convenient accident, or was it a pragmatic symbol with a validity as great as Adams' dualism?

And when one goes to Beauvais or Laon,

what does one see? Structures which are the
greatest engineering feats in human history up to the time of their building. The technicians of the twelfth and thirteenth centuries, far from being traditionalists, were creating an entirely new concept of architecture, dynamic rather than static. In their cathedrals we see a sublime fusion of high spirituality and advanced technology.

Moreover, these are the first vast monuments in all history to be built by free—nay, unionized!—labor. Almost the only branch of technology to make little progress during the Middle Ages was weight-lifting. The freemasons of those centuries, unlike the voiceless slaves and conscript peasants of past ages, would not often be bothered with handling big stones. Both Romanesque and Gothic engineers achieved enormous scale with small blocks. That these churches are filled not only with gifts and monuments of the feudal aristocracy but perhaps to an even greater extent with chapels, windows, and the like offered by the guilds of craftsmen and merchants who dominated the walled cities above which the Virgin's temples towered points to a social revolution closely connected with the technological revolution. And these changes had their roots not merely in economic developments but in religion, which, if vital, can never be divorced from its context.

St. Benedict of Nursia, the founder of the Benedictine Order, is probably the pivotal figure in the history of labor. Greco-Roman society had rested on the backs of slaves. Work was the lot of slaves, and any free man who dirtied his hands with it, even in the most casual way, demeaned himself. Plato once sharply rebuked two friends who had constructed an apparatus to help solve a geometrical problem: they were contaminating thought. Plutarch tells us that Archimedes was ashamed of the machines he had built. Seneca remarks that the inventions of his time, such as stenography, were naturally the work of slaves, since slaves alone were concerned with such things. In the classical tradition there is scarcely a hint of the dignity of labor. The provision of Benedict, himself an aristocrat, that his monks should work in fields and shops therefore marks a revolutionary reversal of the traditional attitude toward labor; it is a high peak along the watershed separating the modern from the ancient world. For the Benedictine monks regarded manual labor not as a mere regrettable necessity of their corporate life but rather as an integral and spiritually valuable part of their discipline. During the Middle Ages the general reverence for the laboring monks did much to increase the prestige of labor and the self-respect of the laborer. Moreover, since the days of St. Benedict every major form of Western asceticism has held that "to labor is to pray," until in its final development under the Puritans, labor in one's "calling" became not only the prime moral necessity but also the chief means of serving and praising God. The importance of frugal living and consecrated labor in building up fluid investment capital and in fostering the rapid expansion of capitalist economy in the regions of Europe and America most deeply affected by the puritan spirit is a commonplace of the economic history of early modern times. The Benedictine ancestry of the puritan attitude toward work is less often emphasized.

Moreover, although St. Benedict had not intended that his monks should be scholars, a great tradition of learning developed in the abbeys following his *Rule:* for the first time the practical and the theoretical were embodied in the same individuals. In Antiquity learned men did not work, and workers were not learned. Consequently, ancient science consisted mostly of observation and abstract thought; experimental methods were rarely used. The craftsmen had accumulated a vast fund of factual knowledge about natural forces and substances, but the social cleavage prevented classical scientists from feeling that stimulus from technology which has been so conspicuous an element in the development of modern experimental science. The monk was the first intellectual to get dirt under his fingernails. He did not immediately launch into scientific investigation, but in his very person he destroyed the old artificial barrier between the empirical and the speculative, the manual and the liberal arts, and thus helped create a social atmosphere favorable to scientific and technological development. It is no accident, therefore, that his ascetic successors, the friar and the Puritan, were eminent and ardent in experiment.

The first power machine, the water wheel,

appeared in the Roman Empire in the last century before Christ; but it may have been a barbarian invention, since we know that by the time of Christ it was already used in northern Denmark and China. Not until after the disintegration of the Western Roman Empire did it become common. By 1086, William the Conqueror's *Domesday Book* shows us that in England there were over 5600 water mills for some 3000 communities. Since there is no reason to believe that Britain was technologically in advance of the Continent, this means that by the end of the eleventh century every European was living daily in the presence of a major engine motored by nonhuman power.

This is the sort of situation that breeds new ideas. From the late tenth century onward, water power gradually began to be applied not only to grinding grain but to all sorts of industrial processes: forging, tanning, making the mash for beer, sawing wood, doing the laundry, polishing armor, and sharpening knives. In cloth-making one of the most tedious and labor-consuming processes was fulling: for ages men had endlessly tramped the raw cloth in troughs filled with water and fuller's earth until it was properly felted. Now hammers powered by water wheels did the job so effectively that in the thirteenth century the English cloth industry shifted from the flat southeast to the more rugged northwest part of the country, where the streams ran a bit faster and good millsites were more available.

The creak of water wheels, then, was a sound

as typical of Henry Adams' age of cathedral building as was the *Ave stella maris* chanted in praise of the Virgin. Was this pure coincidence, or perhaps even the embryonic form of the modern schizophrenia which separates spiritual values from material concerns? The Middle Ages did not seem to think so. St. Bernard's Cistercian monks were so devoted to the Virgin that every one of their hundreds of monasteries was dedicated to her; yet these White Benedictines seem often to have led the way in the use of power. Some of their abbeys had four or five water wheels, each powering a different workshop.

Streams of water were proving most useful; what about the streams of air? In 1185, just at the moment when great Gothic spires were beginning to pierce the sky, the windmill appears, first in Yorkshire. As early as the tenth century there had been crude windmills in eastern Iran, rotating on a vertical axis stuck into the upper millstone. The European windmill, rotating on a horizontal axle and requiring gears, seems to be a separate and certainly far more effective invention. Within seven years, that is by 1192, there were windmills from Germany to Provence, and from Yorkshire to Syria, where the first one was built by Crusaders. The windmill spread as rapidly in the late twelfth and early thirteenth century as moving pictures did in the early twentieth. We know, for example, that in the thirteenth century there were at least 120 windmills in and around the Flemish city of Ypres alone.

All of a sudden what has been called the Age of Faith got an entirely new vision of nature as a reservoir of vast forces to be explored, harnessed, and used according to human need. Gravity had been little exploited, but by 1199 a new type of counterweight artillery had been invented so powerful that the older forms, inherited from the Romans, became obsolete. Water clocks were a nuisance because in cold weather they froze, and many technicians of the thirteenth century began puttering with the idea of a purely mechanical clock activated by weights. By 1271 Robert the Englishman tells us that they had almost cracked the problem, but not quite. By about 1330 two solutions had been found—one north of the Alps and one in Italy—in the invention of two forms of escapement to regulate the flow of force through such machines. In the fourteenth century no municipality of Europe felt that it could hold up its head unless its cathedral or city hall were graced by a monumental clock in which, at the booming of the hours, the kings and prophets of Israel and the locally more admired saints marched and countermarched.

Not only gravity but the force of compressed air and steam began to be investigated, and the emergence in the seventeenth century of steam engines can be shown to have a direct connection with developments four hundred years earlier. Moreover, the thirteenth century began to make gunpowder. At the beginning it was used for simple jet-propulsion—rockets first appear in Europe in 1258 at Cologne—but by 1327 cannons are found. The cannon is a one-cylinder internal-combustion engine, and all modern motors of this type are technically descended from it. In 1661 when Samuel Moreland first tried to substitute a piston for a cannon ball and apply the force to peaceful work, he used powder in his engine; and the conscious analogy of guns continued to handicap the development of internal-combustion machines until the nineteenth century, when liquid fuels were tried.

In terms of Henry Adams' contrast between the Virgin and the dynamo, there is a final item from the thirteenth century which is suggestive. The most vocal, although perhaps not the greatest, scientist of the time was Friar Roger Bacon, whose scientific interests, incidentally, were religiously motivated. Among his contemporaries, Bacon most admired a certain Peter of Maricourt, who lived in Paris and carried on scientific experiments. Presumably he was as devout a Christian as Friar Roger, since he is sometimes called Peter the Pilgrim, implying a pilgrimage to Jerusalem. In 1269 Peter was serving as a military engineer in the service of Charles of Anjou, younger brother of St. Louis of France, at the siege of Lucera, a Muslim city in southern Italy. The siege was boring, so Peter wrote the first treatise on the magnet. The mariner's compass had come into use in the late twelfth century, probably arriving from China. Peter had watched compass-makers at work and had become interested in magnetic phenomena. His recorded observations are the basis of all later study of magnetism. At the end of his little monograph he offers the design of a wheel to be turned perpetually by magnetic force. The fact that it would not work is far less important than the fact that he attempted it. In 1600 when William Gilbert published his great book on the magnet, he consciously rested his work on Peter's; and when, over two hundred years later, Faraday invented the dynamo, he knew his debt to Gilbert. Peter of Maricourt's abortive magnetic wheel is the grandfather of the dynamo.

When Roger Bacon wrote, "Machines may be made by which the largest ships, with only one man steering them, will move faster than if they were filled with rowers; wagons may be built which will move with unbelievable speed and without the aid of beasts; flying machines can be constructed in which a man may beat the air with mechanical wings like a bird . . . ; machines will make it possible for men to go to the bottom of seas and rivers," he was speaking not as a lonely visionary but rather for the technicians of his age. And today we know that these hopes were not fantastic.

Indeed, by Bacon's time the actual accomplishment was great. For two hundred years and more there had already been a rapid replacement of human by nonhuman energy wherever industry demanded large amounts of power or where the required motion was so simple and repetitive that a man could be replaced by a mechanism. The chief glory of the Middle Ages was not, as Henry Adams thought, its cathedrals, its epics, its vast structures of scholastic philosophy, or even its superb music, which Adams' nieces learned to sing for his delectation; it was the building for the first time in history of a complex civilization which was upheld not on the sinews of sweating slaves and coolies but primarily by nonhuman power. The century which achieved the highest expression of the cult of the Virgin Mary likewise first envisaged the concept of a labor-saving power technology which has played so large a part in the formation of the modern world.

This was no accident. In 1953 Margaret Mead went back, after twenty-five years of absence, to visit the primitive but intelligent Manus living on islands near northern New Guinea. She wanted to see what had happened to these few thousand people as a result of their experience during the Second World War, when more than a million American troops passed through their country in the attack against Japan. She found that the Manus had two very definite and related opinions about Americans.

First of all, to them Americans seemed to be people "who treated each other and the Manus with whom they came in contact 'like brothers,' who, in fact, treated their neighbor like themselves in the fundamental sense that he was assumed to be the same kind of guy." Even American racial prejudices seemed to them relatively insignificant: pitch-black themselves, they rejoiced to see black Americans moving with apparent freedom in this novel, friendly world.

And second, the Manus were much impressed by the idea that power machinery could so greatly lighten the burdens of even the poor and subordinate. Miss Mead, who knows their language, quotes one of them as saying, "The Americans believe in having work done by machines so that men can live to old age instead of dying worn out while they are still young." And another: "From the Americans we learned that human beings are irreplaceable and unexpendable, while all material things are replaceable and so expendable." And another: "From the Americans we learned that it is *only* human beings that are important." Admitting that the Manus saw not America but only the American Armed Forces under very special circumstances, Miss Mead states that nevertheless they "shrewdly recognized that the American willingness to sacrifice things for people came from having plenty of things, so many that there were always more, so many because of the apparently inexhaustible productivity of a machine economy, built not upon the limited strength of human beings but upon the unlimited potentialities of machines."

The Virgin and the dynamo are not opposing principles permeating the universe; they are allies. The growth of medieval power technology, which escaped Adams' attention, is a chapter in the conquest of freedom.

More than that, to those who search out "why it happened," it is part of the history of religion. The humanitarian technology which in later centuries has grown from medieval seeds was not rooted in economic necessity; for such "necessity" is inherent in every society, yet has found expression only in the Occident, nourished in the tradition of Western theology. It is ideas which make necessities conscious. The labor-saving power machines of the later Middle Ages were harmonious with the religious assumption of the infinite worth of even the most seemingly degraded human personality, and with an instinctive repugnance toward subjecting any man to a monotonous drudgery which seems less than human in that it requires the exercise neither of intelligence nor of choice. The Middle Ages, believing that the Heavenly Jerusalem contains no temple, began to explore the practical implications of this profoundly Christian paradox. Although to labor is to pray, the goal of labor is to end labor.

We have been too easily impressed by the dualities of Descartes and by the majestic symbols of his disciple, Henry Adams. Closely observed, experience does not in fact fall into neat opposing categories—spirit and matter, religion and technology, man and cosmos, cathedral and powerhouse. Reality is more complex than this, and its parts more intricately interlocked. Man is a bit cosmic; the cosmos is a bit humane; and the free man may worship without despair.

A conversation with Aldous Huxley not infrequently put one at the receiving end of an unforgettable monologue. About a year before his lamented death he was discoursing on a favorite topic: man's unnatural treatment of nature and its sad results. To illustrate his point he told how, during the previous summer, he had returned to a little valley in England where he had spent many happy months as a child. Once it had been composed of delightful grassy glades; now it was becoming overgrown with unsightly brush because the rabbits that formerly kept such growth under control had largely succumbed to a disease, myxomatosis, that was deliberately introduced by the local farmers to reduce the rabbits' destruction of crops. Being something of a Philistine, I could be silent no longer, even in the interests of great rhetoric. I interrupted to point out that the rabbit itself had been brought as a domestic animal to England in 1176, presumably to improve the protein diet of the peasantry.

All forms of life modify their contexts. The most spectacular and benign instance is doubtless the coral polyp. By serving its own ends, it has created a vast undersea world favorable to thousands of other kinds of animals and plants. Ever since man became a numerous species he has affected his environment notably. The hypothesis that his fire-drive method of hunting created the world's great grasslands and helped to exterminate the monster mammals of the Pleistocene from much of the globe is plausible, if not proved. For six millennia at least, the banks of the lower Nile have been a human artifact rather than the swampy African jungle which nature, apart from man, would have made it. The Aswan Dam, flooding 5000 square miles, is only the latest stage in a long process. In many regions terracing or irrigation, over-grazing, the cutting of forests by Romans to build ships to fight Carthaginians or by Crusaders to solve the logistics problems of their expeditions have profoundly changed some ecologies. Observation that the French landscape falls into two basic types, the open fields of the north and the *bocage* of the south and west, inspired Marc Bloch to undertake his classic study of medieval agricultural methods. Quite unintentionally, changes in human ways often affect nonhuman nature. It has been noted, for example, that the advent of the automobile eliminated huge flocks of sparrows that once fed on the horse manure littering every street.

The history of ecologic change is still so rudimentary that we know little about what really happened, or what the results were. The extinction of the European aurochs as late as 1627 would seem to have been a simple case of overenthusiastic hunting. On more intricate matters it often is impossible to find solid information. For a thousand years or more the Frisians and Hollanders have been pushing back the North Sea, and the process is culminating in our own time in the reclamation of the Zuider Zee. What, if any, species of animals, birds, fish, shore life, or plants have died out in the process? In their epic combat with Neptune have the Netherlanders overlooked ecological values in such a way that the quality of human life in the Netherlands has suffered? I cannot discover that the questions have ever been asked, much less answered.

People, then, have often been a dynamic element in their own environment, but in the present state of historical scholarship we usually do not know exactly when, where, or with what effects man-induced changes came. As we enter the last third of the twentieth century, however, concern for the problem of ecologic backlash is mounting feverishly. Natural science, conceived as the effort to understand the nature of things, had flourished in several eras and among several peoples. Similarly, there had been an age-old accumulation of technological skills, sometimes growing rapidly, sometimes slowly. But it was not until about four generations ago that Western Europe and North America arranged a marriage between science and technology, a union of the theoretical and the empirical approaches to our natural environment. The emergence in widespread practice of the Baconian creed that scientific knowledge means technological power over nature can scarcely be dated before about 1850, save in the chemical industries, where it is anticipated in the eighteenth century. Its acceptance as a normal pattern of action may mark the greatest event in human history since the invention of agriculture, and perhaps in nonhuman terrestrial history as well.

Almost at once the new situation forced the crystallization of the novel concept of ecology; indeed, the word *ecology* first appeared in the English language in 1873. Today, less than a century later, the impact of our race upon the environment has so increased in force that it has changed in essence. When the first cannons were fired, in the early fourteenth century, they affected ecology by sending workers scrambling to the forests and mountains for more potash, sulfur, iron ore, and charcoal, with some resulting erosion and deforestation. Hydrogen bombs are of a different order: a war fought with them might alter the genetics of all life on this planet. By 1285 London had a smog problem arising from the burning of soft coal, but our present combustion of fossil fuels threatens to change the chemistry of the globe's atmosphere as a whole, with consequences which we are only beginning to guess. With the population explosion, the carcinoma of planless urbanism, the now geological deposits of sewage and garbage, surely no creature other than man has ever managed to foul its nest in such short order.

There are many calls to action, but specific proposals, however worthy as individual items, seem too partial, palliative, negative: ban the bomb, tear down the billboards, give the Hindus contraceptives and tell them to eat their sacred cows. The simplest solution to any suspect change is, of course, to stop it, or, better yet, to revert to a romanticized past: make those ugly gasoline stations look like Anne Hathaway's cottage or (in the Far West) like ghost-town saloons. The "wilderness area" mentality invariably advocates deep-freezing an ecology, whether San Gimignano or the High Sierra, as it was before the first Kleenex was dropped. But neither atavism nor prettification will cope with the ecologic crisis of our time.

What shall we do? No one yet knows. Unless we think about fundamentals, our specific measures may produce new backlashes more serious than those they are designed to remedy.

As a beginning we should try to clarify our thinking by looking, in some historical depth, at the presuppositions that underlie modern technology and science. Science was traditionally aristocratic, speculative, intellectual in intent; technology was lower-class, empirical, action-oriented. The quite sudden fusion of these two toward the middle of the nineteenth century is surely related to the slightly prior and contemporary democratic revolutions which, by reducing social barriers, tended to assert a functional unity of brain and hand. Our ecologic crisis is the product of an emerging, entirely novel, democratic culture. The issue is whether a democratized world can survive its own implications. Presumably we cannot unless we rethink our axioms.

One thing is so certain that it seems stupid to verbalize it: both modern technology and modern science are distinctively *Occidental.* Our technology has absorbed elements from all over the world, notably from China; yet everywhere today, whether in Japan or in Nigeria, successful technology is Western. Our science is the heir to all the sciences of the past, especially perhaps to the work of the great Islamic scientists of the Middle Ages, who so often outdid the ancient Greeks in skill and perspicacity: ibn-al-Haytham in optics, for example; or Omar Khayyám in mathematics. Indeed, not a few works of such geniuses seem to have vanished in the original Arabic and to survive only in medieval Latin translations that helped to lay the foundation for later Western developments. Today, around the globe, all significant science is Western in style and method, whatever the pigmentation or language of the scientists.

A second pair of facts is less well recognized because they result from quite recent historical scholarship. The leadership of the West, both in technology and in science, is far older than the so-called Scientific Revolution of the seventeenth century or the so-called Industrial Revolution of the eighteenth century. These terms are in fact outmoded and obscure the true nature of what they try to describe—significant stages in two long and separate developments. By 1000 A.D. at the latest—and perhaps, feebly, as much as two hundred years earlier—the West began to apply water power to industrial processes other than milling grain. This was followed in the late twelfth century by the har-

nessing of wind power, as we saw in the previous chapter. From simple beginnings, but
with remarkable consistency of style, the West
rapidly expanded its skills in the development
of power machinery, labor-saving devices, and
automation. Not in craftsmanship but in basic
technological capacity, the Latin West of the
later Middle Ages far outstripped its elaborate,
sophisticated, and aesthetically magnificent
sister cultures, Byzantium and Islam. In 1444
a great Greek ecclesiastic, Bessarion, who had
gone to Italy, wrote a letter to a prince in
Greece. He is amazed by the superiority of
Western ships, arms, textiles, glass. But above
all he is astonished by the spectacle of water
wheels sawing timbers and pumping the bellows
of blast furnaces. Clearly, he had seen nothing
of the sort in the Near East.

By the end of the fifteenth century the technological superiority of Europe was such that
its small, mutually hostile nations could spill
out over all the rest of the world, conquering,
looting, and colonizing. The symbol of this
technological superiority is the fact that Portugal, one of the weakest states of the Occident,
was able to become, and to remain for a century, mistress of the East Indies. And we must
remember that the technology of Vasco da
Gama and Albuquerque was built by pure
empiricism, drawing remarkably little support
or inspiration from science.

In the present-day vernacular understanding, modern science is supposed to have begun
in 1543, when both Copernicus and Vesalius

published their great works. It is no derogation of their accomplishments, however, to point out that such structures as the *Fabrica* and the *De revolutionibus* do not appear overnight. The distinctive Western tradition of science, in fact, began in the late eleventh century with a massive movement of translation of Arabic and Greek scientific works into Latin. A few notable books—Theophrastus, for example—escaped the West's avid new appetite for science, but within less than two hundred years effectively the entire corpus of Greek and Muslim science was available in Latin, and was being eagerly read and criticized in the new European universities. Out of criticism arose new observation, speculation, and increasing distrust of ancient authorities. By the late thirteenth century Europe had seized global scientific leadership from the faltering hands of Islam. It would be as absurd to deny the profound originality of Newton, Galileo, or Copernicus as to deny that of the fourteenth-century scholastic scientists like Buridan or Oresme on whose work they built. Before the eleventh century, science scarcely existed in the Latin West, even in Roman times. From the eleventh century onward, the scientific sector of Occidental culture has increased in a steady crescendo.

Since both our technological and our scientific movements got their start, acquired their character, and achieved world dominance in the Middle Ages, it would seem that we cannot understand their nature or their present impact upon ecology without examining fundamental medieval assumptions and developments.

Until recently, agriculture has been the chief occupation even in "advanced" societies; hence, any change in methods of tillage has much importance. Early plows, drawn by two oxen, did not normally turn the sod but merely scratched it. Thus, cross-plowing was needed, and fields tended to be squarish. In the fairly light soils and semiarid climates of the Near East and Mediterranean, this worked well. But such a plow was inappropriate to the wet climate and often sticky soils of Northern Europe. By the latter part of the seventh century after Christ, however, following obscure beginnings, certain Northern peasants were using an entirely new kind of plow, equipped with a vertical knife to cut the line of the furrow, a horizontal share to slice under the sod, and a moldboard to turn it over. The friction of this plow with the soil was so great that it normally required not two but eight oxen. It attacked the land with such violence that cross-plowing was not needed, and fields tended to be shaped in long strips.

In the days of the scratch plow, fields were distributed generally in units capable of supporting a single family. Subsistence farming was the presupposition. But no peasant owned eight oxen: to use the new and more efficient plow, peasants pooled their oxen to form large plow teams, originally receiving (it would appear) plowed strips in proportion to their contribution. Thus, distribution of land was based no longer on the needs of a family but, rather, on the capacity of a power machine to till the earth. Man's relation to the soil was profoundly changed. Formerly man had been part of nature; now he was the exploiter of nature. Nowhere else in the world did farmers develop any analogous agricultural implement. Is it coincidence that modern technology, with its ruthlessness toward nature, has so largely been produced by descendants of these peasants of Northern Europe?

This same exploitive attitude appears slightly before 830 A.D. in Western illustrated calendars. In older calendars the months were shown as passive personifications. The new Frankish calendars, which set the style for the Middle Ages, are very different: they show men coercing the world around them—plowing, harvesting, chopping trees, butchering pigs. Man and nature are two things, and man is master.

These novelties seem to be in harmony with larger intellectual patterns. What people do about their ecology depends on what they think about themselves in relation to things around them. Human ecology is deeply conditioned by beliefs about our nature and destiny—that is, by religion. To Western eyes this is very evident in, say, India or Ceylon. It is equally true of ourselves and of our medieval ancestors.

The victory of Christianity over paganism was the greatest psychic revolution in the history of our culture. It has become fashionable today to say that for better or worse we live in "the post-Christian age." Certainly the forms

of our thinking and language have largely
ceased to be Christian, but to my eye the substance often remains amazingly akin to that of the past. Our daily habits of action, for example, are dominated by an implicit faith in perpetual progress which was unknown either to Greco-Roman Antiquity or to the Orient. It is rooted in, and is indefensible apart from, Judeo-Christian teleology. The fact that Communists share it merely helps to show what can be demonstrated on many other grounds: that Marxism, like Islam, is a Judeo-Christian heresy. We continue today to live, as we have lived for about 1700 years, very largely in a context of Christian axioms.

What did Christianity tell people about their relations with the environment?

While many of the world's mythologies provide stories of creation, Greco-Roman mythology was singularly incoherent in this respect. Like Aristotle, the intellectuals of the ancient West denied that the visible world had had a beginning. Indeed, the idea of a beginning was impossible in the framework of their cyclical notion of time. In sharp contrast, Christianity inherited from Judaism not only a concept of time as nonrepetitive and linear but also a striking story of creation. By gradual stages a loving and all-powerful God had created light and darkness, the heavenly bodies, the earth and all its plants, animals, birds, and fishes. Finally, God had created Adam and, as an afterthought, Eve to keep man from being lonely. Man named all the animals, thus establishing his dominance over them. God planned all of this explicitly for man's benefit and rule: no item in the physical creation had any purpose save to serve man's purposes. And, although man's body is made of clay, he is not simply part of nature: he is made in God's image.

Especially in its Western form, Christianity is the most anthropocentric religion the world has seen. As early as the second century both Tertullian and St. Irenaeus of Lyons were insisting that when God shaped Adam he was foreshadowing the image of the incarnate Christ, the Second Adam. Man shares, in great measure, God's transcendence of nature. Christianity, in absolute contrast to ancient paganism and Asia's religions (except, perhaps, Zoroastrianism), not only established a dualism of man and nature but also insisted that it is God's will that man exploit nature for his proper ends.

At the level of the common people this worked out in an interesting way. In Antiquity every tree, every spring, every stream, every hill had its own *genius loci,* its guardian spirit. These spirits were accessible to men, but were very unlike men; centaurs, fauns, and mermaids show their ambivalence. Before one cut a tree, mined a mountain, or dammed a brook, it was important to placate the spirit in charge of that particular situation, and to keep it placated. By destroying pagan animism, Christianity made it possible to exploit nature in a mood of indifference to the feelings of natural objects.

It is often said that for animism the Church substituted the cult of saints. True; but the cult of saints is functionally quite different from animism. The saint is not *in* natural objects; he may have special shrines, but his citizenship is in heaven. Moreover, a saint is entirely a man; he can be approached in human terms. In addition to saints, Christianity of course also had angels and demons inherited from Judaism and perhaps, at one remove, from Zoroastrianism. But these were all as mobile as the saints themselves. The spirits *in* natural objects, which formerly had protected nature from man, evaporated. Man's effective monopoly on spirit in this world was confirmed, and the old inhibitions to the exploitation of nature crumbled.

When one speaks in such sweeping terms, a note of caution is in order. Christianity is a complex faith, and its consequences differ in differing contexts. What I have said may well apply to the medieval West, where in fact technology made spectacular advances. But the Greek East, a highly civilized realm of equal Christian devotion, seems to have produced no marked technological innovation after the late seventh century, when Greek fire was invented. The key to the contrast may perhaps be found in a difference in the tonality of piety and thought which students of comparative theology find between the Greek and the Latin Churches. The Greeks believed that sin was intellectual blindness, and that salvation was found in illumination, orthodoxy — that is, clear thinking. The Latins, on the other hand, felt that sin was moral evil, and that salvation was to be found in right conduct. Eastern theology has been intellectualist. Western theology has been voluntarist. The Greek saint contemplates; the Western saint acts. The implications of Christianity for the conquest of nature would emerge more easily in the Western atmosphere.

The Christian dogma of creation, which is found in the first clause of the Creeds, has another meaning for our comprehension of today's ecologic crisis. By revelation, God had given man the Bible, the Book of Scripture. But since God had made nature, nature also must reveal the divine mentality. The religious study of nature for the better understanding of God was known as natural theology. In the early Church, and always in the Greek East, nature was conceived primarily as a symbolic system through which God speaks to men: the ant is a sermon to sluggards; rising flames are the symbol of the soul's aspiration. This view of nature was essentially artistic rather than scientific. While Byzantium preserved and copied great numbers of ancient Greek scientific texts, science as we conceive it could scarcely flourish in such an ambience.

However, in the Latin West by the early thirteenth century natural theology was following a very different bent. It was ceasing to be the decoding of the physical symbols of God's communication with man and was becoming the effort to understand God's mind by discovering how his creation operates. The rainbow was no longer simply a symbol of hope first sent to Noah after the Deluge: Robert Grosseteste, Friar Roger Bacon, and Theodoric of Freiberg produced startlingly sophisticated work on the optics of the rainbow, but they did it as a venture in religious understanding. From the thirteenth century onward into the eighteenth, every major scientist, in effect, explained his motivations in religious terms. Indeed, if Galileo had not been so expert an amateur theologian he would have got into far less trouble: the professionals resented his intrusion. It was not until the late eighteenth century that the hypothesis of God became unnecessary to many scientists.

It is often hard for the historian to judge, when men explain why they are doing what they want to do, whether they are offering real reasons or merely culturally acceptable reasons. The consistency with which scientists during the long formative centuries of Western science said that the task and the reward of the scientist were "to think God's thoughts after him" leads one to believe that this was their real motivation. If so, then modern Western science was cast in a matrix of Christian theology. The dynamism of religious devotion, shaped by the Judeo-Christian dogma of creation, gave it impetus.

We would seem to be headed toward conclusions unpalatable to many Christians. Since both *science* and *technology* are blessed words in our contemporary vocabulary, some may be happy at the notions, first, that, viewed historically, modern science is an extrapolation of natural theology and, second, that modern technology is at least partly to be explained as an Occidental, voluntarist realization of the Christian dogma of man's transcendence of, and rightful mastery over, nature. But, as we now recognize, somewhat over a century ago science and technology, hitherto quite separate activities, joined to give mankind powers which, to judge by many of the ecologic effects, are out of control. If so, Christianity bears a huge burden of guilt.

I personally doubt that disastrous ecologic backlash can be avoided simply by applying to our problems more science and more technology. Our science and technology have grown out of Christian attitudes toward man's relation to nature which are almost universally held not only by Christians and neo-Christians but also by those who fondly regard themselves as post-Christians. Despite Copernicus, all the cosmos rotates around our little globe. Despite Darwin, we are *not,* in our hearts, part of the natural process. We are superior to nature, contemptuous of it, willing to use it for our slightest whim. A governor of California, like myself a churchman but less troubled than I, spoke for the Christian tradition when he said (as is alleged), "When you've seen one redwood tree, you've seen them all." To a Christian a tree can be no more than a physical fact. The whole concept of the sacred grove is alien to Christianity and to the ethos of the West. For nearly two millennia Christian missionaries have been chopping down sacred groves, which are idolatrous because they assume spirit in nature.

What we do about ecology depends on our ideas of the man-nature relationship. More science and more technology are not going to get us out of the present ecologic crisis until we find a new religion, or rethink our old one. The beatniks and hippies, who are the basic revolutionaries of our time, show a sound instinct in their affinity for Zen Buddhism and Hinduism, which conceive of the man-nature relationship as very nearly the mirror image of the Christian view. These faiths, however, are as deeply conditioned by Asian history as Christianity is by the experience of the West, and I am dubious of their viability among us.

Possibly we should ponder the greatest radical in Christian history since Christ: St. Francis of Assisi. The prime miracle of St. Francis is the fact that he did not end at the stake, as many of his left-wing followers did. He was so clearly heretical that a General of the Franciscan Order, St. Bonaventura, a great and perceptive Christian, tried to suppress the early accounts of Franciscanism. The key to an understanding of Francis is his belief in the virtue of humility, not merely for the individual but for man as a species. Francis tried to depose man from his monarchy over creation and set up a democracy of all God's creatures. With him the ant is no longer simply a homily for the lazy, flames a sign of the thrust of the soul toward union with God; now they are Brother Ant and Sister Fire, praising the Creator in their own ways as Brother Man does in his.

Later commentators have said that Francis

preached to the birds as a rebuke to men who would not listen. The records do not read so; he urged the little birds to praise God, and in spiritual ecstasy they flapped their wings and chirped rejoicing. Legends of saints, especially the Irish saints, had long told of their dealings with animals but always, I believe, to show their human dominance over creatures. With Francis it is different. The land around Gubbio in the Apennines was being ravaged by a fierce wolf. St. Francis, says the legend, talked to the wolf and persuaded him of the error of his ways. The wolf repented, died in the odor of sanctity, and was buried in consecrated ground.

What Sir Steven **Runciman** calls "the Franciscan doctrine of the animal soul" was quickly stamped out. Quite possibly it was in part inspired, consciously or unconsciously, by the belief in reincarnation held by the Cathar heretics who at that time teemed in Italy and southern France, and who presumably had got it originally from India. It is significant that at just the same moment, about 1200, traces of metempsychosis are found also in Western Judaism, in the Provençal *Cabbala*. But Francis held neither to transmigration of souls nor to pantheism. His view of nature and of man rested on a unique sort of pan-psychism of all things animate and inanimate, designed for the glorification of their transcendent Creator, who, in the ultimate gesture of cosmic humility, assumed flesh, lay helpless in a manger, and hung dying on a scaffold.

I am not suggesting that many contemporary

Americans who are concerned about our ecologic crisis will be either able or willing to
counsel with wolves or exhort birds. However,
the present increasing disruption of the global
environment is the product of a dynamic technology and science which were originating in
the Western medieval world and against which
St. Francis was rebelling in so original a way.
Their growth cannot be understood historically
apart from distinctive attitudes toward nature
which are deeply grounded in Christian dogma. The fact that most people do not think of
these attitudes as Christian is irrelevant. No
new set of basic values has been accepted in our
society to displace those of Christianity. Hence
we shall continue to have a worsening ecologic
crisis until we reject the Christian axiom that
nature has no reason for existence save to serve
man.

The greatest spiritual revolutionary in Western history, St. Francis, proposed what he
thought was an alternative Christian view of
nature and man's relation to it: he tried to substitute the idea of the equality of all creatures,
including man, for the idea of man's limitless
rule of creation. He failed. Both our present
science and our present technology are so
tinctured with orthodox Christian arrogance
toward nature that no solution for our ecologic crisis can be expected from them alone.
Since the roots of our trouble are so largely
religious, the remedy must also be essentially
religious, whether we call it that or not. We
must rethink and refeel our nature and destiny.

94 The profoundly religious, but heretical, sense of the primitive Franciscans for the spiritual autonomy of all parts of nature may point a direction. I propose Francis as a patron saint for ecologists.

About a hundred and thirty years ago Auguste Comte schematized human history in terms of three ages: the age of religion, the age of philosophy, and the age of positive knowledge or science. He had faith in science, and his positivism is the heart of modern orthodoxy. All of us today take for granted that humanity is progressing from bondage to mastery of the natural environment, from superstition to knowledge, from darkness to light. It is axiomatic that science is the exploration of an endless frontier and that its processes cannot be reversed or even seriously interrupted. Every American or European, every Asian or African deeply influenced by Western culture has implicit trust in the inevitability and rightness of this onward sweep of science. Even the churches embrace the new orthodoxy, if they are judged more by what they do not say than by what they say.

The modern positivist is a man of faith as much as was the medieval mystic. The concept of human destiny secularized by Comte was evolved by Joachim of Flora, a Cistercian abbot of the late twelfth century, who divided history according to the Trinitarian dogma, equating the ages of the Father, the Son, and the Holy Ghost with an age of fear, an age of love, and an age of freedom. Joachim's vision was taken up by the left wing of the Franciscan movement and broadcast over Europe. It was inherent in the thinking of late medieval and early modern proletarian revolutions and underlies the Marxist straight-line notion of human destiny. When Comte transmuted Joachim's formula, he was replacing one faith with another closely related to it.

No faith can afford to reign unexamined. Our habit of regarding scientific progress as inevitable may in fact be dangerous to its continuing vigor. In every civilized society something that can legitimately be called science has existed, but the amount of energy put into it has varied enormously. In every age minds of great ability are attracted to the focus of cultural interest, be it the fine arts, literature, religion, science, or something else. If the cultural climate shifts, the concentration of intellectual energies and capital investments follows.

Science must have a positive emotional context to thrive, as well as economic and political encouragement. Legislatures and corporate bodies must reach decisions favorable to science, and investors and voters must approve what their representatives do. Parents must want science in the education of their children. Above all, a significant proportion of the ablest minds must choose to dedicate themselves with passion to scientific investigation if the movement is to progress.

The modern outburst of scientific activity is not necessarily permanent. The cultural support that science enjoys today rests more on fear of foreign enemies and of disease than upon understanding, and fear may not be a healthy or lasting foundation. Science needs its statesmen, and statesmanship demands the long view. The future of science, like its past, will be largely a matter of accident unless measures to assure its continuance are attentively sought. Since the energy that civilization expends on any activity depends on the cultural climate, the important question for scientists today is: What can be done to ensure an affirmative social context for science?

The historian has no ready answers. History does not foretell the future, but study of the past may provide some keys to understanding. Viewing human experience in vastly different circumstances helps to dislodge presuppositions, and may free our ideas about what needs to be done to assure the future of science.

The prestige of science among us sustains a common but false assumption that any robust culture must have had considerable scientific activity. Rome was immensely vigorous. Languages descended from Latin are still spoken from Tijuana to Bucharest. The overwhelming mass of legal structures of the world, not only in Europe but in Asia and the Communist countries as well, is descended from Roman law. The Romans had vast creative ability and originality; yet there was no ancient Roman science. Nothing that can be called science existed in the Latin tongue until near the twelfth century. From our modern point of view, Roman indifference to Greek science was spectacular. It has been argued that by the time of the Roman Empire Greek science was so far past its great days that it could not attract the vigorous

Roman mind. But distinguished Greek scientists, such as Galen, lived for long periods in Rome. As for the "petering out" of Hellenic science, one of the most original Greek scientific thinkers, Philoponus of Alexandria, was contemporary with Justinian in the sixth century. Greek science was available to the Romans, but was ignored.

Even more disconcerting is the case of Islamic science. During some four centuries, from roughly 750 A.D. to 1150, Islam held the lead in scientific activity. In the eighth century a government-supported institute of translation emerged in Baghdad. Very nearly the complete corpus of Greek science and a major part of Indian science were made available in Arabic within about eighty years. Original scientific work began appearing in Arabic by the late ninth century, especially in mathematics, optics, astronomy, and medicine.

In the early tenth century al-Rāzī, an Islamic physician, produced a book known eventually in Latin as *Liber continens,* an encyclopedic codification of Greek and Hindu medicine, including a great deal of al-Rāzī's own observation. It is probably the biggest single book ever written by a medical man, and is a superb work. In 1279 it was translated into Latin for Charles of Anjou by a Jewish physician of Agrigento in Sicily. It was published in Brescia in 1486 and reprinted four times before 1542. It was a fundamental medical reference book for centuries, and was entirely absorbed into the stream of Western medicine. But perhaps the most striking thing about it is that no complete copy of al-Rāzī's great medical encyclopedia exists in Arabic. It was practically forgotten in Islam after a few generations.

The Arabic-speaking civilization knew what science was and was proficient in it. For four hundred years science was one of its major concerns. But a crystallization of other values occurred in the late eleventh century which shifted the whole focus of Islamic culture. Science was abandoned, and abandoned deliberately.

Christianity's relation to scientific activity has varied greatly through the ages. It has been said that early Christianity killed Greek science; but Christians were no more indifferent to science than were contemporary pagan Romans. The early Christian attitude was based on the view that natural phenomena were relatively unimportant. Only spiritual values had significance. The natural world deserved attention solely because God used it to communicate specific messages to the faithful.

The concept of the function and nature of the physical world is illustrated in a sixth-century story about Pope Gregory the Great. Gregory, not yet Pope, had seen English slaves in the Roman slave markets, and decided to evangelize this pagan people. He received permission from the then Pope and started for England. On the evening of the second day out, while he was resting and reading, a locust —*locusta* in Latin—hopped up on his book. He knew that God was speaking to him. The Latin words *loco sta* mean "stop"; he took this to be the meaning of the message and went no farther. The next day couriers from Rome reached him and summoned him back. The people of Rome had demanded that the Pope recall Gregory from what would have been a lifelong mission because they desperately needed his leadership.

It is plain that science could not flourish in a culture that held to such a "rebus" interpretation of natural phenomena. But by the twelfth century this attitude began to change, at least in the Latin West. People began to pay more attention to the physical world. Sculpture of the early Gothic period clearly shows that the artist looked at real vegetation when he carved ornamental leaves or flowers. As we have seen, in the thirteenth century St. Francis of Assisi supplemented the doctrine that material things convey messages from God with the new idea that natural phenomena are important in themselves: all things are fellow creatures praising God in their own ways, as men do in theirs. This new notion opened a door to objective examination of nature and partly explains the enthusiasm for experimental science in the Franciscan order at that time.

Another concept crucial for the whole development of modern science was emphasized in the thirteenth century and found its clearest spokesman in the Franciscan friar Roger Bacon. He said that there are two sources of knowledge of the mind of God—the Book of

Scripture and the Book of Nature—and that each of these must be searched by the faithful with equal energy. He pointed out further that study of the Book of Nature had been sorely neglected.

This idea, natural theology, changed the role of men from passive recipients of spiritual messages through natural phenomena to active seekers for an understanding of the divine nature as it is reflected in the pattern of creation. Natural theology was the motivational basis of late medieval and early modern science. Every major scientist from about 1250 to about 1650, four hundred years during which our present scientific movement was taking form, considered himself also a theologian: Leibnitz and Newton are notable examples. The importance to science of the religious devotion which these men gave their work cannot be exaggerated.

Why did the idea of an operational natural theology emerge in the thirteenth century, and in the Latin West alone? There was no similar development in Greek Christendom. It may have sprung from the key religious struggle of the time, the battle of Latin Christianity with the great Cathar heresy. Early in the thirteenth century it looked as though the Cathars were going to get control of a strip of territory extending from the middle Balkans across northern Italy and southern France almost to the Atlantic coast, separating the Papacy from the more orthodox areas of northern Europe. The Cathars' major doctrine was that there are two gods—a god of good and a god of evil. The visible universe is the creation of the god of evil, which means that living a good life involves having as little as possible to do with physical actuality. Christianity holds that matter is the creation of the one good Deity. In the process of upholding the Christian position against Catharism, natural theology assumed a new relevance and vividness.

Natural theology was unquestionably a major underpinning of Western science. By the time the theological motivation began to diminish, Western science was formed. Today the motive force of natural theology has long been spent, and it does not seem to have been replaced with any other idea of equal power. Are modern scientists quite sure why they are pursuing science? Science is fun, and the exhilaration of the chase may keep it going for a long while. But will scientific advance continue without more serious impulsion?

Scientists and the general public must become increasingly aware of the complexity and intimacy of science's relationships to its total context. The modern tendency to regard science as somehow apart from, or even dominant over, the main human currents that surround it is dangerous to its continuance, and can be harmful even to progress within science. The veneration of the circle is an example of a general presupposition that constricted even so great a scientific mind as Galileo's. Galileo, in bondage to the axiom that the circle is the perfect curved form and therefore necessary to any significant speculation, could not seriously contemplate Kepler's thesis that the planets move in elliptical orbits. He neither accepted nor refuted Kepler's notion. He committed the unforgivable sin: he disregarded it.

Fixation on the circle was almost complete in ancient culture. The Romans recognized only three ovoid forms: in arenas, in shields, and in the bezels of rings. Pagan Scandinavians used the oval for a type of brooch, but discarded it as soon as they were Christianized—that is, Mediterraneanized. The Middle Ages had no oval forms except occasionally the nimbus surrounding Christ in scenes of the Last Judgment or the Ascension, and even this was usually a version of the ancient Christian fish symbol, pointed at both ends. As late as the fifteenth century, artists could not draw a picture of the Colosseum which showed it oval. The first ascertainable oval design in a major European work of art is the paving that Michelangelo designed in 1535 for the remodeling of the Capitoline Piazza in Rome. Michelangelo and his successors during the next fifty years created an atmosphere in which ovoid forms became respectable, until finally Baroque art was dominated by the oval. Kepler's astronomical breakthrough was prepared by the artists who softened up the circle and made variations of the circular form not only artistically but also intellectually acceptable.

While the sanctity of the circle long impeded science by closing avenues of speculation, another inherited classical idea of a very different sort restrained progress by divorcing thought from practice. As has been noted earlier, manual labor was extolled for seven hundred years by monks, especially the Benedictines, as being not merely expedient but spiritually valuable as well. With the late medieval revival of Greek and Roman attitudes, however, the classical contempt for manual labor reasserted itself. The universities emerging in the thirteenth century had faculties in the liberal arts, law, theology, and medicine. Medicine was the only discipline with an embarrassing manual aspect, and in order to retain their prestige the medics separated surgery from medicine. Surgeons did not want to be downgraded either, so surgery became largely theory. There are pictures showing a professor of medicine lecturing to students, while a theoretical surgeon in turn directs a barber surgeon who dissects the cadaver. Medicine advanced during the latter Middle Ages, but it seems likely that it advanced less rapidly than would have been the case if the study of surgery, anatomy, and medicine had been carried on by the same people. Speculation too far removed from substance is often of limited value. The trend to purge university curricula of "vocational" courses may contain a seed of decay.

Current discussion of the problems of maintaining scientific progress usually focuses on the importance of providing an adequate economic base for science and creating an atmosphere of political and intellectual freedom in which science may flourish. But, as we have seen, changes in science in the past have also to be related to changes in basic religious attitudes, in aesthetic perceptions, and in social relationships. More of our attention should be directed to an examination of the sources of our faith in science today, and to the well-springs of motivation that lead men to pursue science. These are not entirely economic or political.

Our science itself may contain unexamined axioms, like the circular prison that held Galileo captive. Hypnotism is an example of a phenomenon that science has not really tried to explicate, apparently because in some way it seems outside accepted categories of "reality," although it has been used in amazing ways in dentistry and surgery. A distinguished surgeon told me about a delicate heart operation carried out under hypnotism and added, "That sure is fooling them." But who is being fooled?

The continuation of civilization as we know it depends on science, and the continuance of science would seem to depend on our ability to examine this sphere of human activity objectively and relate it to its human context. Those responsible for the statesmanship of science must develop a scientific understanding of science itself. They must become increasingly aware of the intricacy of the ecology of the scientist. We must learn to think about science in new ways unless we intend to leave the future of science to chance.

The most obvious thing, although perhaps not the basic thing, that today is changing and affecting much else by its change is technology. Yet the rapidly growing literature on the nature of technological innovation and its relation to other activities is still largely rubbish because so few of the relevant concrete facts have thus far been ascertained. It is an inverted pyramid of generalities, the apex of which is very nearly a void. The five plump volumes of *A History of Technology,* edited under the direction of Charles Singer, give the layman a quite false impression of the state of knowledge. They are useful as a starting point, but they are almost as much a codification of error as of sound information. It is to be feared that the physical weight of these books will be widely interpreted as the weight of authority and that philosophers, sociologists, and others whose personal researches do not lead them into the details of specific technological items may continue to be deceived as to what is known.

Since man is a hypothesizing animal, there is no point in calling for a moratorium on speculation in this area of thought until more firm facts can be accumulated. Indeed, such a moratorium, even if it were possible, would slow down the growth of factual knowledge because hypothesis normally provokes counterhypotheses, and then all factions adduce facts in evidence, often new facts. The best that we can do at present is to work hard to find the facts and then to think cautiously about the facts which have been found.

In view of our ignorance, then, it would seem wise to discuss the problems of the nature, the motivations, the conditioning circumstances, and the effects of the act of invention far less in terms of generality than in terms of specific instances about which something seems to be known.

The beginning of wisdom may be to admit that even when we know some facts in the history of technology, these facts are not always fully intelligible—that is, capable of "explanation"—simply because we lack adequate contextual information. The Chumash Indians of the coast of Santa Barbara County built plank boats which were unique in the pre-Columbian New World: their activity was such that the Spanish explorers of California named a Chumash village "La Carpintería." A map will show that this tribe had a particular inducement to venture upon the sea: they were enticed by the largest group of offshore islands along the Pacific Coast south of Canada. But why did the tribes of South Alaska and British Columbia, of Araucanian Chile, or of the highly accidented Eastern coast of the United States never respond to their geography by building plank boats? Geography would seem to be only one element in explanation. To be sure, the Chumash coast is one of the few Pacific areas where there are seepages of tarlike petroleum good for calking plank boats. But if one has never seen such a boat, this use is not obvious.

Can a plank-built East Asian boat have drifted on the great arc of currents in the North Pacific to the Santa Barbara region? It is entirely possible; but such boats would have been held together by pegs, whereas the Chumash boats were lashed, like the dhows of the Arabian Sea or the early Norse ships. Diffusion seems improbable.

Since a group can conceive nothing which is not first conceived by a person, we are left with the hypothesis of a genius: a Chumash Indian who at some unknown date achieved a breakaway from log dugout and reed balsa to the plank boat. But the idea of "genius" is itself an ideological artifact of the age of the Renaissance when painters, sculptors, and architects were trying to raise their social status above that of craftsmen. Does the notion of genius "explain" Chumash plank boats? On the contrary, it would seem to be no more than a traditionally acceptable way of labeling the great Chumash innovation as unintelligible. All we can do is to observe the fact of it and hope that eventually we may grasp the meaning of it.

A symbol of the rudimentary nature of our thinking about technology, its development, and its human implications, is the fact that while the *Encyclopaedia Britannica* has an elaborate article on "Alphabet," thus far it contains no discussion of its own organizational presupposition, alphabetization. Alphabetization is the basic invention for the storage and recovery of information; it is fully comparable in significance to the Dewey decimal system and to the new electronic devices for these purposes. Modern big business, big government, big scholarship are inconceivable without alphabetization. One hears that the chief reason why the Chinese Communist regime has decided to Romanize Chinese writing is the inefficiency of trying to classify everything from telephone books to tax registers in terms of 214 radicals of ideographs. Yet we are so blind to the nature of our technical equipment that the world of Western scholars, which uses alphabetization constantly, has produced scarcely the beginning of a history of it.

Fortunately, Sterling Dow of Harvard University is engaged in the task. He believes that the earliest evidence of alphabetization is found in Greek materials of the third century B.C. In other words, there was a thousand-year gap between the invention of the alphabet as a set of phonetic symbols and the realization that these symbols, and their sequence in individual written words, could be divorced from their phonetic function and used for an entirely different purpose: an arbitrary but very useful convention for storage and retrieval of verbal materials. That we have neglected thus completely the effort to understand so fundamental an invention should give us humility whenever we try to think about the larger aspects of technology.

Coinage was one of the most significant and rapidly diffused innovations of late Antiquity. The dating of it has recently become more conservative than formerly: the earliest extant

coins were sealed into the foundation of the
temple of Artemis at Ephesus about 600 B.C., and the invention of coins—that is, lumps of metal the value of which is officially certified — was presumably made in Lydia not more than a decade earlier.

Here we seem to know something, at least until the next archaeological spades turn up new testimony. But what do we know with any certainty about the impact of coinage? We are compelled to tread the slippery path of *post hoc ergo propter hoc*. There was a great acceleration of commerce in the Aegean, and it is hard to escape the conviction that this movement, which is the economic presupposition of the Periclean Age, was lubricated by the invention of coinage.

If we dare to go this far, we may venture further. Why did the atomic theory of the nature of matter appear so suddenly among the philosophers of the Ionian cities? Their notion that all things are composed of different arrangements of identical atoms of some "element," whether water, fire, ether, or something else, was an intellectual novelty of the first order, yet its sources have not been obvious. The psychological roots of atomism would seem to be found in the saying of Heraclitus of Ephesus that "all things may be reduced to fire, and fire to all things, just as all goods may be turned into gold and gold into all goods." He thought that he was just using a metaphor, but the metaphor had been possible for only a century before he used it.

Here we are faced with a problem of critical

method. Apples had been dropping from trees for a considerable period before Newton discovered gravity: we must distinguish cause from occasion. But the appearance of coinage is a phenomenon of a different order from the fall of an apple. The unprecedented element in the general life of sixth-century Ionia, the chief stimulus to the prosperity which provided leisure for the atomistic philosophers, was the invention of coinage: the age of barter was ended. Probably no Ionian was conscious of any connection between this unique new technical instrument and the brainstorms of the local intellectuals. But that a causal relationship did exist can scarcely be doubted, even though it cannot be "proved" but only perceived.

Fortunately, however, there are instances of technological devices of which the origins, development, and effects outside the area of technology are quite clear. A case in point is the pennon.

The stirrup is first found in India in the second century B.C. as the big-toe stirrup. For climatic reasons its diffusion to the north was blocked, but it spread wherever India had contact with barefoot aristocracies, from the Philippines and Timor on the east to Ethiopia on the west. The nuclear idea of the stirrup was carried to China on the great Indic culture wave which also spread Buddhism to East Asia, and by the fifth century the shod Chinese were using a foot stirrup.

The stirrup made possible, although it did

not require, a new method of fighting with the
lance. The unstirruped rider delivered the
blow with the strength of his arm. But stirrups,
combined with a saddle equipped with pommel
and cantle, welded rider to horse. Now the
warrior could lay his lance at rest between his
upper arm and body: the blow was delivered
not by the arm but by the force of a charging
stallion. The stirrup thus substituted horsepower for man-power in battle.

The increase in violence was tremendous.
So long as the blow was given by the arm, it was
almost impossible to impale one's foe. But in
the new style of mounted shock combat, a good
hit might put the lance entirely through his
body and thus disarm the attacker. This would
be dangerous if the victim had friends about.
Clearly, a baffle must be provided behind the
blade to prevent penetration by the shaft of
the lance and thus permit retraction.

Some of the Central Asian peoples attached
horse tails behind the blades of lances—this
was probably being done by the Bulgars before
they invaded Europe. Others nailed a piece of
cloth, or pennon, to the shaft behind the blade.
When the stirrup reached Western Europe
about 730 A.D., an effort was made to meet the
problem by adapting to military purposes the
old Roman boar spear which had a metal crosspiece behind the blade precisely because boars,
bears, and leopards had been found to be so
ferocious that they would charge up a spear
not so equipped.

This was not, however, a satisfactory solution. The new violence of warfare demanded heavier armor. The metal crosspiece of the lance would sometimes get caught in the victim's armor and prevent recovery of the lance. By the early tenth century, Europe was using the Central Asian cloth pennon, since even if it got entangled in armor it would rip and enable the victor to retract his weapon.

Until our dismal age of camouflage, fighting men have always decorated their equipment. The pennons on lances quickly took on color and design. A lance was too long to be taken into a tent conveniently, so a knight usually set it upright outside his tent, and if one were looking for him, one looked first for the flutter of his familiar pennon. Knights riding held their lances erect, and since their increasingly massive armor made recognition difficult, each came to be identified by his pennon. It would seem that it was from the pennon that distinctive "connoissances" were transferred to shield and surcoat. And with the crystallization of the feudal structure, these heraldic devices became hereditary, the symbols of status in European society.

In battle, vassals rallied to the pennon of their liege lord. Since the king was, in theory if not always in practice, the culmination of the feudal hierarchy, his pennon took on a particular aura of emotion: it was the focus of secular loyalty. Gradually a distinction was made between the king's two bodies, his person and his "body politic," the state. But a colored cloth on the shaft of a spear remained the primary symbol of allegiance to either body, and so remains even in polities which have abandoned monarchy. The grimly functional rags first nailed to lance shafts by Asian nomads have had a great destiny. But it is no more remarkable than that of the cross, a hideous implement in the Greco-Roman technology of torture, which was to become the chief symbol of the world's most widespread religion.

In tracing the history of the pennon, and of many other technological items, there is a temptation to convey a sense of inevitability. However, a novel technique merely offers opportunity; it does not command. As has been mentioned, the big-toe stirrup reached Ethiopia. It was still in common use there in the nineteenth century, but at the present time Muslim and European influences have replaced it with the foot stirrup. However, travelers tell me that the Ethiopian gentleman, whose horse is equipped with foot stirrups, rides with only his big toes resting in the stirrups.

Indeed, in contemplating the history of technology, and its implications for our understanding of ourselves, one is as frequently astonished by blindness to innovation as by insights of invention. The Hellenistic discovery of the helix was one of the greatest of technological inspirations. Very quickly it was applied not only to gearing but also to the pumping of water by the so-called Archimedes screw. Somewhat later the holding screw appears in both Roman and Germanic metalwork. The helix was taken for granted thenceforth in Western technology.

Yet, despite the sophistication of the Chinese in many technical matters, no form of helix was known in East Asia before modern times: it reached India but did not pass the Himalayas. Indeed, I have not been able to locate any such device in the Far East before the early seventeenth century when Archimedes screws, presumably introduced by the Portuguese, were used in Japanese mines.

Next to the wheel, the crank is probably the most important single element in machine design, yet until the fifteenth century the history of the crank is a dismal record of inadequate vision of its potentialities. It first appears in China under the Han dynasty, applied to rotary fans for winnowing hulled rice, but its later applications in the Far East were not conspicuous. In the West the crank seems to have developed independently and to have emerged from the hand quern. The earliest querns were fairly heavy, with a handle, or handles, inserted laterally in the upper stone, and the motion was reciprocating. Gradually the stones grew lighter and thinner, so that it was harder to insert the peg-handle horizontally: its angle creeps upward until eventually it stands vertically on top. All the querns found at the Saalburg had horizontal handles, and it is increasingly clear that the vertical peg is post-Roman.

Seated before a quern with a single vertical handle, a person of the twentieth century would give it a continuous rotary motion. It is far from clear that one of the very early Middle Ages would have done so. Crank motion was a kinetic invention more difficult than we can easily conceive. Yet at some point before the time of Louis the Pious the sense of the appropriate motion changed; for out of the rotary quern came a new machine, the rotary grindstone, which (as the Latin term for it, *mola fabri,* shows) is the upper stone of a quern turned on edge and adapted to sharpening. Thus, in Europe at least, crank motion was invented before the crank, and the crank does not appear before the early ninth century. As for the Near East, I find not even the simplest application of the crank until al-Jazarī's book on automata of 1206 A.D.

Once the simple crank was available, its development into the compound crank and connecting rod might have been expected quite quickly. Yet there is no sign of a compound crank until 1335, when the Italian physician of the Queen of France, Guido da Vigevano, in a set of astonishing technological sketches, illustrates three of them. By the fourteenth century, Europe was using crankshafts with two simple cranks, one at each end. Guido was interested in the problem of self-moving vehicles: paddlewheel boats and fighting towers propelled by windmills or from the inside. For such constricted situations as the inside of a boat or a tower it apparently occurred to him to consolidate the two cranks at the ends of the crankshaft into a compound crank in its middle. It was an inspiration of the first order, yet nothing came of it. Evidently the Queen's physician, despite his technological interests, was socially too far removed from workmen to influence the actual technology of his time. The compound crank's effective appearance was delayed for another three generations, as we noted previously (page 17). Thereafter the idea spread like wildfire, and European applied mechanics was revolutionized.

How can we understand the lateness of the discovery, whether in China or Europe, of even the simple crank, and then the long delay in its wide application and elaboration? Continuous rotary motion is typical of inorganic matter, whereas reciprocating motion is the sole movement found in living things. The crank connects these two kinds of motion; therefore we who are organic find that crank motion does not come easily to us. The great physicist and philosopher Ernst Mach noticed that infants find crank motion hard to learn. Despite the rotary grindstone, even today razors are whetted rather than ground: we find rotary motion a bar to the greatest sensitivity. Perhaps as early as the tenth century the hurdy-gurdy was played with a cranked resined wheel vibrating the strings. But by the thirteenth century the hurdy-gurdy was ceasing to be an instrument for serious music. It yielded to the reciprocating fiddle bow, an introduction of the tenth century from Java which became the foundation of modern European musical development. To use a crank, our tendons and muscles must relate themselves to the motion of galaxies and electrons. From this inhuman adventure our race long recoiled.

A sequence originally connected with the

crank may serve to illustrate another type of problem in the act of technological innovation: the fact that a simple idea transferred out of its first context may have a vast expansion. The earliest appearance of the crank, as has been mentioned, is found on Han-dynasty rotary fans to winnow husked rice. The identical apparatus appears in the eighteenth century in the Palatinate, in upper Austria and the Siebenbürgen, and in Sweden. I have not seen the exact channel of this diffusion traced, but it is clearly part of the general Jesuit-inspired *chinoiserie* of Europe in that age. I strongly suspect, but cannot demonstrate, that all subsequent rotary blowers, whether in furnaces, dehydrators, wind tunnels, air-conditioning systems, or the simple electric fan, are descended from this Han machine, which seems, in China itself, to have produced no progeny.

Doubtless when scholarship in the history of technology becomes firmer, another curious device will illustrate the same point. To judge by its wide distribution, the fire piston is an old invention in Malaya. Thomas Kuhn of Princeton, who has made careful studies of the history of our knowledge of adiabatic heat, assures me that when the fire piston appeared in late eighteenth-century Europe not only for laboratory demonstrations but as a commercial product to light fires, there is no hint in the purely scientific publications that its inspiration was Malayan. But the scientists, curiously, also make no mention of the commercial fire pistons then available. So many Europeans, especially Portuguese and Netherlanders, had been trading, fighting, ruling, and evangelizing in the East Indies for so long a time before the fire piston is found in Europe that it is hard to believe that the Malayan fire piston was not observed and reported. The realization of its potential in Europe was considerable, culminating in the diesel engine.

Why are such nuclear ideas sometimes not exploited in new and wider applications? What sorts of barriers prevent their diffusion? Why, at times, does what appeared to be a successful technological item fall into disuse? The history of the faggoted forging method of producing sword blades may assist our thinking about such questions.

In late Roman times, north of the Alps, Celtic, Slavic, and Germanic metallurgists began to manufacture swords with laminations made by welding together bundles of rods of different qualities of iron and steel, hammering the resulting strip thin, folding it over, welding it all together again, and so on. In this way a fairly long blade was produced which had the cutting qualities of steel but the toughness of iron. Although such swords were used at times by barbarian auxiliaries in the Roman army, the Roman legions never adopted them. Yet as soon as the Western Empire crumbled, the short Roman stabbing sword vanished and the laminated slashing blade alone held the field of battle. Can this conservatism in military equipment have been one reason for the failure of the Empire to stop the Germanic invasions? The Germans had adopted the new type of blade with enthusiasm, and by Carolingian times were manufacturing it in quantities in the Rhineland for export to Scandinavia and to Islam, where it was much prized. Yet, although such blades were produced marginally as late as the twelfth century, for practical purposes they ceased to be used in Europe in the tenth century. Does the disappearance of such sophisticated swords indicate a decline in medieval metallurgical methods?

We should be cautious in crediting the failure of the Romans to adopt the laminated blade to pure stupidity. The legions seem normally to have fought in very close formation, shield to shield. In such a situation, only a stabbing sword could be effective. The Germans at times used a "shield wall" formation, but it was probably a bit more open than the Roman and permitted use of a slashing sword. If the Romans had accepted the new weapon, their entire drill and discipline would have been subject to revision. Unfortunately, we lack studies of the development of Byzantine weapons sufficiently detailed to let us judge whether, or to what extent, the vigorously surviving Eastern Roman Empire adapted itself to the new military technology.

The famous named swords of Germanic myth, early medieval epic, and Wagnerian opera were laminated blades. They were produced by the vast patience and skill of smiths who themselves became legendary. Why did they cease to be made in any number after the tenth century? The answer is found in the rapid increase in the weight of European armor as a result of the consistent Frankish elaboration of the type of mounted shock combat made possible by the stirrup. After the turn of the millennium a sword in Europe had to be very nearly a club with sharp edges: the best of the earlier blades was ineffective against such defenses. The faggoted method of forging blades survived and reached its technical culmination in Japan, where, thanks possibly to the fact that archery remained socially appropriate to an aristocrat, mounted shock combat was less emphasized than in Europe and armor remained lighter.

Let us now turn to a different problem connected with the act of invention. How do methods develop by the transfer of ideas from one device to another? The origins of the cannon ball and the cannon may prove instructive.

Hellenistic and Roman artillery were activated by the torsion of cords. This was reasonably satisfactory for summer campaigns in the Mediterranean basin, but north of the Alps and in other damper climates the cords tended to lose their resilience. In 1004 A.D. a radically different type of artillery appeared in China with the name *huo p'ao*. It consisted of a large sling-beam pivoted on a frame and actuated by men pulling in unison on ropes attached to the short end of the beam away from the sling. It first appears outside China in a Spanish Christian illumination of the early twelfth century, and from this one might assume diffusion through Islam. But its second appearance is in the northern Crusader army attacking Lisbon in 1147, where a battery of them were operated by shifts of one hundred men for each. It would seem that the Muslim defenders were quite unfamiliar with the new engine of destruction and soon capitulated. This invention, therefore, appears to have reached the West from China not through Islam but directly across Central Asia. Such a path of diffusion is the more credible because by the end of the same century the magnetic needle likewise arrived in the West by the northern route, not as an instrument of navigation but as a means of ascertaining the meridian, and Western Islam got the compass from Italy. When the new artillery arrived in the West it had lost its name. Because of structural analogy, it took on a new name borrowed from a medieval instrument of torture, the ducking stool, or *trebuchetum*.

Whatever its merits, the disadvantages of the *huo p'ao* were the amount of man-power required to operate it and the fact that since the gang pulling the ropes would never pull with exactly the same speed and force, missiles could not be aimed with great accuracy. The problem was solved by substituting a huge counterweight at the short end of the sling-beam for the ropes pulled by men. With this device a change in the weight of the caisson of stones or earth, or else a shift of the weight's position in relation to the pivot, would modify the range of the projectile and then keep it uniform, permitting concentration of fire on one spot in the fortifications to be breeched. Between 1187 and

1192 an Arabic treatise written in Syria for Saladin mentions not only Arab, Turkish, and Frankish forms of the primitive trebuchet, but also credits to Iran the invention of the trebuchet with swinging caisson. This ascription, however, may be in error; for from about 1220 onward Oriental sources frequently call this engine *magribī*—that is, "Western." Moreover, while the counterweight artillery has not yet been documented for Europe before 1199, it quickly displaced the older forms of artillery in the West, whereas this new and more effective type of siege machinery became dominant in the Mameluke army only in the second half of the thirteenth century. Thus the trebuchet with counterweights would appear to be a European improvement on the *huo p'ao*. Europe's debt to China was repaid in 1272 when, if we may believe Marco Polo, he and a German technician, helped by a Nestorian Christian, delighted the Great Khan by building trebuchets which speedily reduced a besieged city.

But the very fact that the power of a trebuchet could be so nicely regulated impelled Western military engineers to seek even greater exactitude in artillery attack. They quickly saw that until the weight of projectiles and their friction with the air could be kept uniform, artillery aim would still be variable. As a result, as early as 1244 stones for trebuchets were being cut in the royal arsenals of England calibrated to exact specifications established by an engineer; in other words, the cannon ball before the cannon.

The germinal idea of the cannon is found in the metal tubes from which, at least by the late ninth century, the Byzantines had been shooting Greek fire. It may be that even so early they were also shooting rockets of Greek fire, propelled by the expansion of gases, from bazooka-like metal tubes. When, shortly before 673, the Greek-speaking Syrian refugee engineer Callinicus invented Greek fire, he started the technicians not only of Byzantium but also of Islam, China, and eventually the West in search of ever more combustible mixtures. As chemical methods improved, the saltpeter often used in these compounds became purer, and combustion tended toward explosion. In the thirteenth century one finds, from the Yellow Sea to the Atlantic, incendiary bombs, rockets, firecrackers, and fireballs shot from tubes like Roman candles. The flame and roar of all this have made it marvelously difficult to ascertain just when gunpowder artillery, shooting hard missiles from metal tubes, appeared. The first secure evidence is a famous English illumination of 1327 showing a vase-shaped cannon discharging a giant arrow. Moreover, our next certain reference to a gun, a *"pot de fer à traire garros de feu"* at Rouen in 1338, shows how long it took for technicians to realize that the metal tube, gunpowder, and the calibrated trebuchet missile could be combined. However, iron shot appear at Lucca in 1341; in 1346 in England there were two calibers of lead shot; and balls appear at Toulouse in 1347.

The earliest evidence of cannon in China is

an extant example of 1332. It is not necessary to assume the miracle of an almost simultaneous independent Chinese invention of the cannon: enough Europeans were wandering the Yuan realm to have carried it eastward. And it is very strange that the Chinese did not develop the cannon further. Neither India nor Japan knew cannon until the sixteenth century when they arrived from Europe. As for Islam, despite several claims to the contrary, the first certain use of gunpowder artillery by Muslims comes from Cairo in 1366 and Alexandria in 1376; by 1389 it was common in both Egypt and Syria. Thus there was roughly a forty-year lag in Islam's adoption of the European cannon.

Gunpowder artillery, then, was a complex invention which synthesized and elaborated elements drawn from diverse and sometimes distant sources. Its impact upon Europe was equally complex. Its influences upon other areas of technology such as fortification, metallurgy, and the chemical industries are axiomatic, although they demand much more exact analysis than they have received. The increased expense of war affected tax structures and governmental methods; the new mode of fighting helped to modify social and political relationships. All this has been self-evident for so long a time that perhaps we should begin to ask ourselves whether the obvious is also the true.

For example, it has often been maintained that a large part of the new physics of the seventeenth century sprang from concern with military ballistics. Yet there was continuity between the thought of Galileo or Newton and the fundamental challenge to the Aristotelian theory of impetus which appeared in Franciscus de Marchia's lectures at the University of Paris in the winter of 1319–1320, seven years before our first evidence of gunpowder artillery. Moreover, the physicists both of the fourteenth and of the seventeenth centuries were to some extent building upon the criticisms of Aristotle's theory of motion propounded by Philoponus of Alexandria in the age of Justinian, a time when I can detect no new technological stimulus to physical speculation. While most scientists have been aware of current technological problems, and have often talked in terms of them, both science and technology seem to have enjoyed a certain autonomy in their development.

It may well be that continued examination will show that many of the political, economic, and social as well as intellectual developments in Europe which have traditionally been credited to gunpowder artillery were in fact taking place for quite different reasons. But we know of one instance in which the introduction of firearms revolutionized an entire society: Japan.

Metallurgical skills were remarkably high in Japan when, in 1543, the Portuguese brought both small arms and cannon to Kyushu. Japanese craftsmen quickly learned from the gunsmiths of European ships how to produce such weapons, and within two or three years were turning them out in great quantity. Military tactics and castle construction were rapidly revised. Nobunaga and his successor, Hideyoshi, seized the new technology of warfare and utilized it to unify all Japan under the shogunate. In Japan, in contrast to Europe, there is no ambiguity about the consequences of the arrival of firearms. But from this fact we must be careful not to argue that the European situation is equally clear if only we would see it so.

In examining the origins of gunpowder artillery, we have seen that its roots are multiple, but that all of them (save the European name *trebuchet*) lie in the soil of military technology. It would appear that each area of technology has a certain self-contained quality: borrowings across craft lines are not as frequent as might be expected. Yet they do occur, if exceptionally. A case in point is the fusee.

In the early fifteenth century, clock-makers tried to develop a portable mechanical timepiece by substituting a spring drive for the weight which powered stationary clocks. But this involved entirely new problems of power control. The weight on a clock exerted equal force at all times, whereas a spring exerts less force in proportion as it uncoils. A new escapement was therefore needed which would exactly compensate for this gradual diminution of power in the drive.

Two solutions were found, the stackfreed and the fusee, the latter being the more satisfactory. Indeed, a leading historian of horology has said of the fusee: "Perhaps no problem in mechanics has ever been solved so simply and so perfectly." Its first appearance was about 1449. The fusee equalizes the changing force of the mainspring by means of a brake of gut or fine chain which is gradually wound spirally around a conical axle, the force of the brake being dependent upon the leverage of the radius of the cone at any given point and moment. It is a device of great mechanical elegance. Yet the idea did not originate with the clock-makers: they borrowed it from the military engineers. In Konrad Keyser's monumental treatise on the technology of warfare, *Bellifortis,* completed in 1405, we find such a conical axle in an apparatus for spanning a heavy crossbow. With very medieval humor, this machine was called "the virgin," presumably because it offered least resistance when the bow was slack and most when it was taut.

In terms of eleven specific technological acts, or sequences of acts, we have been pondering an abstraction, the act of technical innovation. It is quite possible that there is no such thing to ponder. The analysis of the nature of creativity is one of the chief intellectual commitments of our age. Just as the old unitary concept of "intelligence" is giving way to the notion that the individual's mental capacity consists of a large cluster of various and varying factors mutually affecting each other, so "creativity" may well be a lot of things and not one thing.

Thirteenth-century Europe invented the sonnet as a poetic form and the functional button as a means of making civilized life more nearly possible in boreal climes. Since most of

us are educated in terms of traditional humanistic presuppositions, we value the sonnet but
think 'that a button is just a button. It is doubtful whether the chilly Northerner who invented
the button could have invented the sonnet then
being produced by his contemporaries in Sicily.
It is equally doubtful whether the type of talent
required to invent the rhythmic and phonic relationships of the sonnet pattern is the type
of talent needed to perceive the spatial relationships of button and buttonhole. For the
button is not obvious until one has seen it, and
perhaps not even then. The Chinese never
adopted it: they got no further than to adapt the
tie cords of their costumes into elaborate loops
to fit over cord-twisted knobs. When the Portuguese brought the button to Japan, the Japanese were delighted with it and took over not
only the object itself but also its Portuguese
name. Humanistic values, which have been cultivated historically by very specialized groups
in quite exceptional circumstances, do not encompass sufficiently the observable human values. The billion or more mothers who, since the
thirteenth century, have buttoned their children snugly against winter weather might perceive as much spirituality in the button as in
the sonnet and feel more personal gratitude to
the inventor of the former than of the latter.
And the historian, concerned not only with art
forms but with population, public health, and
what S. C. Gilfillan long ago identified as "the
coldward course" of culture, must not slight
either of these very different manifestations of

what would seem to be very different types of
creativity.

There is, indeed, no reason to believe that technological creativity is unitary. The unknown Syrian who, in the first century B.C., first blew glass was doing something vastly different from his contemporary who was building the first water-powered mill. For all we now know, the kinds of ability required for these two great innovations are as different as those of Picasso and Einstein would seem to be.

The school of physical anthropologists who maintain that *Homo* is *sapiens* because he is *faber*, that his biological differentiation from the other primates is best understood in relation to toolmaking, are doubtless exaggerating a provocative thesis. *Homo* is also *ludens, orans,* and much else. But if technology is defined as the systematic modification of the physical environment for human ends, it follows that a more exact understanding of technological innovation is essential to our self-knowledge, including the ends that are human.

Like any other community, the worldwide
fellowship of intellectuals has its folklore — that
is, things so commonly said that they are commonly believed. Bavarian peasants know that
if you write the magic square

```
S   A   T   O   R
A   R   E   P   O
T   E   N   E   T
O   P   E   R   A
R   O   T   A   S
```

on a piece of paper, and then tear the paper
into tiny bits and mix them with a dog's food,
it is a first-rate vermifuge as well as a notable
example of applied humanism. They also tell
you that some mushrooms are edible whereas
others are poisonous. Intellectuals can segre-
gate these bits of information quite easily into
folk superstition on the one hand and folk
wisdom on the other. But intellectuals have
more difficulty screening the folklore of their
own group.

On the surface, these days we discuss many
things: nuclear power and the problem of con-
trolling it in a world of sovereign states; the
tidal wave of population and how to stem it
without violating individual dignity; the widen-
ing gulf between the industrial nations and
those "emerging," and whether it can be
bridged without wiping out all cultural dis-
tinctiveness; the surge toward abstraction and
subjectivity in all the arts as well as in philosophy, and the problem of renewing communica-

tion between artist and philosopher on the one hand, and their publics, on the other; the approach to a classless culture in the economically advanced nations, and the question whether this is the prelude to an age of faceless conformists. The substratum of all of these questions is: Are humanistic values viable in a world more and more dominated not so much by science as by applied science, by technology? Must the miracle of the person succumb to the order of the computer?

But even the new, and newly trite, metaphors of the humanists are drawn from science and technology. Everyone at times feels that the present explosion of specialized knowledge, not only in the natural sciences but also in humanistic disciplines and the social sciences, is a hydrogen bomb blasting the unity of the human intellect. As the universal cliché has it, we know "more and more about less and less." Just as astronomers, studying the "red shift," tell us that each galaxy is drawing away from every other galaxy and retreating into its own lonely infinity, so with the speed of light human minds are losing contact with each other. Our thinking has got spread over so vast a range of things that it is suffering excess intellectual entropy. Wistfully we yearn for new Aristotles and Leonardos, well knowing that if they could return they would be as appalled as we at the new chaos of what once seemed the mind's cosmos.

Talk about such matters is permeated by a folklore of dualistic demonism. We take it for granted that technology is a way of thinking and acting that is separate from, and hostile to, the humanistic effort to understand and foster the highest human values. Since humanists generally are more skilled and prolific in the use of words than are scientists and engineers, most of what is said is said somberly.

Despondency is so fashionable nowadays that to sketch a sunnier prospect seems philistine. The source of the current gloom, however, is less the objective facts than a subjective fact: to wit, that our inherited intellectual processes, emotional attitudes, and vocabulary are no longer of much use for analyzing and interpreting the spiritual revolution going on all around us. We like to say that "education is learning to think." The truth is that education is learning to think in ways traditionally approved. The new world in which we live is so unlike the past, even the past that is close to us, that in proportion as we are saturated in the Western cultural tradition we are incapacitated for looking clearly at our actual situation and thinking constructively about it. The better we are educated, the more we are fitted to live in a world that no longer exists.

Ours is not the first age in which a once valid kind of education has become not only irrelevant but dangerous because of its irrelevance. The Roman senatorial aristocracy had an almost exclusively rhetorical education. In the days of Cicero and Caesar such schooling had enabled the Roman leaders to debate issues in the Senate with great clarity, and then to implement decisions for the conquest and rule of the Mediterranean. But the letters of Apollinaris Sidonius, Ausonius, or Symmachus fifteen generations later show Roman aristocrats so miseducated in a revered cultural tradition that they could not formulate or discuss the living and entirely novel issues of the age of the Germanic invasions and the Christian mutation. Fortunately they were, at times, better than their education: Sidonius ended up as Bishop of Clermont, leading his people on the walls of the city in successful defense against a besieging Visigothic host.

Once more, in our own century, change has been rapid and basic but education and conceptual patterns have lagged. The old ideas often do not help us to understand and cope with the new situations. As a result there is a widespread sense of frustration among educated people because their expectation is so at variance with their experience. Quite naturally the gap is verbalized as disintegration and decay.

Such morose pontification, however, is based on a very limited selection among the facts of our time. The full view of the facts justifies not gloom but exhilaration. Our instinct for survival is proving stronger than our education. Like Sidonius we are *doing* better than we *think*. To my eyes, the facts fall into three general sets.

The first of these is the *move toward the center*. The explosion of knowledge and the speed of the trend toward specialization have produced a compensatory swing toward intellectual generality. This is best seen in education for the professions. It has become a commonplace that what a professional student learns in graduate school is largely obsolete by the time he gets his diploma. His training is of little continuing use unless it is combined with understanding of very broad areas related to his professional activity. Only by being more than a specialist can he remain an adequate specialist.

Medical education is a prime example. The general practitioner is a vanishing type: the bright young fellows in the white coats focus on specific organs or diseases. But equally, perhaps more, significant is the fact that whereas the old-fashioned general practitioner was graduated, as a rule, from a medical school physically removed and intellectually insulated from larger academic organisms, a considerable majority of the medical schools established in the United States since the Second World War have been set up as integral parts of the campuses of large universities. The top professionals in the medical world are nearly unanimous that physicians and surgeons should be educated today in intimate conjunction with the whole range of the sciences, the social sciences, and even the humanities.

Similarly, while law schools were once encapsulated, content with their traditional concerns, they are now reaching out to relate themselves, by joint appointment of professors and in other ways, to philosophy, political science, history, sociology, and the other professional schools. Business schools, which even a few years ago were largely factories producing bland young corporation executives, are now much more sophisticated organizations studying social psychology, electronic systems, data processing, and a vast variety of matters far removed from their original functions but involving them with other parts of their universities. Schools for training teachers, so long looking inward at teaching methods, have suddenly turned outward toward the substance of what is taught. Divinity schools, striving to educate a clergy capable of understanding and meeting the spiritual needs of our time, have vastly diversified their interests. Led by the Julliard School of Music in New York, which concluded that musicians must also be educated persons and therefore developed a wide offering in the liberal arts, our conservatories of music, art, theater, and the dance either have become more than technical schools or else have joined with universities providing the studies needed to amplify the intellectual vision of their students.

Related to all this is the current growth of adult education, and, at the highest level, of postdoctoral study. Much of this is stimulated by the swift obsolescence of information and skills. More of it, however, rests on the mounting conviction that the best professional is best because he is more than a professional; that the essential skill is a capacity for getting an overview of what one is doing and for achieving abstraction from it and mobility in relation to its accepted presuppositions and methods.

Intense specialization, then, is only one aspect of the intellectual revolution of our time. Equally significant is a massive gravitation toward common concerns. This is not something that *should* happen: it *is* happening on a stupendous scale involving huge investments of capital and human devotion. The move toward the center is fundamental to our thinking about ourselves and our time.

The second major pattern of intellectual growth, as I see it, is closely related to the first: it is *recognition that technology and science are, and always have been, integral to the human adventure,* and not things curiously alien from the concerns of our race.

It is said that after the ceremonies dedicating the great telescope on Mount Palomar, someone remarked to an astronomer, "Modern astronomy certainly makes man look insignificant, doesn't it?" To which the astronomer replied, "But man is the astronomer!"

Nothing in nature that a scientist can study is more significant or puzzling than that part of nature that is the scientist himself. Why does he bother to become a scientist? Having bothered, why does he act as he does? How do the structures of his culture shape his work as a scientist, and vice versa? Until very recent years the history of science—which is to say, the scientific examination of the scientist—has been amazingly neglected. But within the last decade or so it has begun to win wider recognition. Even more recent and sudden is the worldwide growth of interest in technology as something to be understood as a human activity if we are to have total access to ourselves as spiritual beings. In 1958 the Society for the History of Technology was established, with a quarterly journal, in the United States. During the past few years new centers for the history of technology have been set up in Europe, especially in France and Italy. We have now begun to mine the veins of humanistic insight awaiting us in the substance not only of pure science but also of technology. Even humanists educated in traditional patterns have generally admitted that Gutenberg's invention, for example, had humanistic implications. It is only recently, however, that we have begun to understand and get excited about the inside technical details of the creative process by which this skilled metallurgist brought his arts to bear on a complex problem and thus produced a device essential to the democratic revolution of our age.

Which brings me to the third pattern in the movement of thought in our generation: *the building of a democratic culture* that expands, supplements, and modifies profoundly our inherited aristocratic culture. The problem we face is very like that which faced the Roman Empire when Christianity became religiously dominant and demanded not a junking of the inherited pagan culture but rather a reworking of it in terms of new presuppositions.

Education has always been largely functional in intent, and in the past it has done two things for society: it has taught the aristocracy how to rule; and it has helped to stabilize the social structure by giving students a distinctive intellectual costume which separated them from those who were not aristocrats. These costumes were often of great elegance and are of continuing aesthetic value. The inertia of our educational systems is such that we will still enjoy the company of many clothed in knee breeches, tricornes and swords, some in hauberks, and a few almost in togas.

In the past the aristocracy has patronized certain activities in which aristocrats themselves have seldom participated intensively, and which therefore have not generally been part of aristocratic education. These were science (apart from mathematics), technology, and the creative arts. They all involved using the hands and thus were beneath the dignity of the educated man. Today in the industrial nations, however, we are far advanced in building a political and economic democracy which already has destroyed the old use of physical costumes to distinguish social classes. We are now unifying our mental costumes. We are pushing on to break the barriers between types of human experience and kinds of values, barriers which, viewed historically, were largely social. Quite unconsciously, for the most part, we are on the way toward building a new sort of humanism that encompasses in its sympathies all kinds of creativity, including those involving hands as well as brains.

Just to give one concrete example: immense scholarly energy has been expended on Machiavelli, Ficino, or Valla, and one begrudges none of it. Yet how many educated people realize that fifteenth-century Italy produced innovations in machine design that in their own way are quite comparable with the Renaissance achievements in other fields? Few of the extant notebooks of Italian engineers prior to Leonardo have been published. I have examined some of the manuscripts, and find in then an excitement, an originality, and an implication for the life of our race during the five hundred years since then that make them the match of any body of material traditionally revered and studied. The building of a democratic culture to crown our political and economic democracy is not a matter of scrapping the treasures of the aristocratic past (although some recasting is inevitable) but rather of understanding *all* aspects of the human enterprise including those traditionally little admired because they were marginal to the aristocracy.

The move toward the center; the recognition that science and technology are integral to mankind's adventure; the building of a democratic culture: these are clearly only three aspects of one thing that is occurring—the achievement of a unity of human knowledge and experience such as no earlier age has imagined. I decline to bewail gathering gloom, the stagnation of excess entropy. The evidence of my eyes shows me a tide of the mind that is the exact reverse.

Because governments must find engineering answers to so many problems, engineers and scientists interested in practical applications of science are fast growing in power at every level of government. In big corporations, more and more men trained as engineers are sitting on the board of directors as well as holding administrative posts. An ever larger number of the world's decisions, touching all of life, are being made by engineers in terms of engineering objectives and values.

More and more people are wondering whether the growing dominance of engineers may threaten other human values, or perhaps even nonhuman values which it would be inhuman to disregard. Decisions made by highway engineers aimed simply at efficient transport have physically split once unified communities, or have destroyed landscapes and historic landmarks. Despite protests, agricultural technicians continue to encourage the use of pesticides to the point where entire species of birds, insects, and even animals are threatened with extinction. Is it a legitimate sentiment, or just sentimentalism, to want to preserve a functioning community or a "useless" bird?

No group in our society seems more disturbed about such questions than engineers themselves. This is not, however, just a matter of conscience; it is a matter of cool-eyed professionalism. Technicians today are realizing that to do their jobs well they must do them in a far wider context of understanding than was once thought necessary. An engineer is judged by his success, but the definition of success is becoming more elaborate. Now that engineering is involved in every phase of mankind's existence, the expert engineer must also be a humanist; he must try to understand life as a totality. The professional fact is that an engineer is increasingly threatened with technical obsolescence in proportion as he is not also a humanist.

Yet those who are trying hardest to add a larger humanistic component to the education of engineering students are often intimidated by too great respect for humanism in its present state. They schedule a course here and a lecture there; the young men read a bit of Plato or of George Orwell, and look at drawings by Matisse. None of this is bad, but it lacks impact. This is partly because it has so little relation to the motivations of most engineering students, who have not yet achieved a professional grasp of the complexity of the problems they will face. But it is chiefly because the present changing condition of humanism is not understood.

Many engineers, and scientists as well, are almost pathetically eager to have humanists help them broaden their vision. What they do not realize is that most humanists are in much the same sort of constricted situation, and perhaps even more blind to their own limitations.

After all, until very recently, education, as 145
Engineers
and the
Making of
a New
Humanism distinct from mere literacy, was almost always reserved for the thin upper crust of society. Humanism quite naturally was shaped by the interests of its clients, and since these excluded anything which involved working with the hands, most humanists disregarded the very important human values of technology and experimental science.

By all means let's read Plato and enjoy Matisse. But curriculum-tinkering is going to remain superficial until more engineers become vividly aware of the new atmosphere. Once engineers have clearly recognized the new mood of the intellectual life of our time, they will transcend their present sense of cultural inferiority and the traditional humanism. They will then be infused with the spirit of humanism rather than embellished with borrowed ornament.

Thanks to electronics, the search for new materials, and the like, there has been a rapid shift in engineering toward the more abstract forms of mathematics, physics, and chemistry. Novel disciplines such as space medicine are bringing similar rapprochements between engineering and both the biological sciences and psychology. Concern over automation and the fact that so many engineers find themselves getting into administrative jobs have led to a surge of interest in engineering circles toward economics, politics, and sociology. Development programs, so largely technological, in the emerging nations have made some understanding of cultural anthropology vividly functional to many engineers. Architecture and regional planning involve whole categories of values traditionally neglected by engineering schools.

Few engineering schools have kept pace with the intellectual advance of the best of their own graduates. As they modify their educational structures to meet the newer professional needs of engineers, they will feel increasingly the shift toward common human concerns, and this in itself will promote humanistic attitudes.

When this happens, engineers will wake up to the fact that engineering has humanistic functions of the highest order. Engineers bear an intellectual — almost a moral — responsibility to make their activities understandable to those who are not engineers, as well as to themselves. They must join vigorously with a small but growing group of professional humanistic scholars to build a bridge between their traditionally separate activities. That bridge is the history of technology and science, a kind of study in which the engineers or scientists can see people like themselves doing things they understand for reasons which they understand. By learning their involvements in the general philosophical, artistic, religious, political, economic, and social milieus of their times, engineers can come more easily to grasp, and to be concerned with, their own ecology.

To many professional engineers, such study will open a portal to the exploration of the human spirit. Yet so long as engineers think of this as no more than an intellectual adventure

for themselves, they will be less than human-147
Engineers
and the
Making of
a New
Humanism
ized. Engineers have as much to give to humanists as to get from them. To one like myself,
not an engineer, the history of technology is as
absorbing, enlightening, and profoundly humanizing as the study of literature. My own
search into it has led me to see categories of
value, kinds of human originality or perversity,
connections or barriers, and sorts of forces
molding our destiny which seem less easily
accessible in any other study.

The obligation of engineers to understand
themselves as engineers, and to share that
understanding with the rest of us, is related to
a final and fundamental matter of morality.

One mark of a mature profession is consciousness of its own history. A second and
equally important sign, however, is conscious
dedication to an explicit ideal goal, a con-
siousness which pervades the teaching of those
who intend to go into the profession. Medical
men are dedicated by their ancient oath to the
liberation of mankind from the ills of the flesh.
Lawyers are committed to liberation from in-
justice. The academic profession is devoted to
liberation from ignorance. The clergy is consecrated to liberating man from the self.

By this criterion, engineering is still an im-
mature profession. One suspects that the mil-
lennial delay of engineers in arriving at such
self-awareness is rooted in the fact that, from
the beginning, the immediate job in hand was
so often either slaughter or profit; the context
did not favor thinking about ultimate prob-

lems. Today engineering is on the verge of professional consciousness of its dedication. Achievement of this is fundamental to the humanizing of engineering.

Engineers are, and always have been, implicitly dedicated to the liberation of mankind from the limitations of the physical world. Their two great coordinate enterprises have been the conquest of matter and the conquest of energy, these involving the conquest of space by communication and transport and the conquest of time by the saving of human labor. Whatever its specific abuses, technology is a profoundly spiritual form of thought and of action. It has flourished best in the context of the presupposition that the physical universe was created for a good purpose, that it is not to be disregarded or transcended, but rather that it is to be treasured and controlled as the necessary ground of psychic life. Even in the early Middle Ages, Western culture began to demonstrate an astonishing technological dynamism. Indeed, the technological leadership of the Occident antedates by several centuries its scientific leadership.

Growing exponentially, Western technology has now led to the globalizing of human experience and the smashing of the physical barriers between peoples. This is the prerequisite to breaking through the other barriers between them. Whatever the incidental problems, it is a prime spiritual achievement. In the industrial nations, technology has likewise led to an increase in the standard of living and of educa-

149
Engineers
and the
Making of
a New
Humanism

tion which has broken the old functional division between educated rulers and uneducated workers. Engineering today is pushing over the geographical and social fences which have prevented mankind from unifying its total experience and thus discovering itself not as classes or tribes but as humanity.

Engineers are the chief revolutionaries of our time. Their implicit ideology is a compound of compassion for those suffering from physical want, combined with a Promethean rebellion against all bonds, even bonds to this planet. Engineers are arch-enemies of all who, because of their fortunate position, resist the surge of the mass of mankind toward a new order of plenty, of mobility, and of personal freedom. Within the societies which have consolidated about the Marxist and the Western democratic revolutions, engineers' activities are the chief threat to surviving privilege.

Without deliberate intent, but by the nature of their activity, engineers have largely destroyed the contemporary validity of the older aristocratic humanism which was a cultural weapon in the hands of the ruling class. When engineers in greater numbers come to know explicitly what they are doing, when they recognize their dedication, they can join with alert humanists to shape a new humanism which will speak for and to a global democratic culture.

The good life is built of an alloy of action and contemplation. In our excessively activist age, there are those who are contemptuous of what they call "spectator sports" and who insist that everyone join all the teams. But this is a caricature of the legitimate existentialist ideal of *l'homme engagé*. Everybody can't cook every meal: there should be someone to compliment the chef.

The relation of action to contemplation is curious and a bit one-sided. Many of us who love music tend to sing off pitch. Few who recognize a good novel when they read it can write a good novel. But the reverse situation seems to be abnormal: I have never heard of a musician who did not profoundly enjoy a great variety of music, or of a poet who did not revel in the work of at least a select few poets, often far removed from their own time, place, and style. Yet it is my impression that most engineers, while they find deep satisfaction and sense of creativity in the *doing* of engineering, seldom have experienced the related but very different pleasures of *contemplating* engineering. I am not speaking of the scrutiny of patent reports to see whether one's bright idea has been forestalled, or of looking at a bridge because one wants to build a better bridge. I mean the enjoyment of engineering by the professional engineer in the mood in which an ultramodern composer who himself experiments with electronic musical instruments can immerse himself in a concert of sixteenth-century madrigals.

This failure to contemplate is deplorable for technicians because it means that they are having less fun in life than they deserve. For the rest of us it is also sad, since unless the professionals in a field habitually ponder their field as well as operate in it, nonprofessionals on the outside have a harder time in understanding it: they need the insights of the doers to help them. Not every art critic can paint a picture; not every political theorist is a practicing lawyer or politician. Nevertheless, if lawyers, diplomats, physicians, clergymen, and artists of every sort had not built up a tradition for the intellectual enjoyment of their fields quite apart from their personal efforts in them, the level of culture would be far lower than it is because the nonspecialist would be much handicapped in trying to share what they have created.

Engineers can double their fun by learning how to enjoy engineering not only actively but also contemplatively, in the mood of a banker who loves numismatics. Numismatics is not just coin-collecting: it can be very cerebral indeed. The invention of money in Asia Minor during the seventh century B.C. provided a basic mutation in the history of commerce because it offered an abstract measure of the value of goods. For the next two thousand years or more, shifts in the nature and metallic content of coins, in their iconography and in their distribution give us information on economic trends, political developments, the state of the fine arts, and the location and nature of trade routes much of which can be got from no other source. Clearly, the study of numismatics will not make a banker a better banker in the purely technical sense; but it can scarcely fail to add to his exhilaration in life. And the fact that he deals daily, as a professional, in the manipulation of commercial values increases the probability that he will understand some things about the tradition of money which would be less evident to those of us whose connection with banking is normally at the level of an overdrawn checkbook. Similarly, the contemplation of engineering as an aspect of the human adventure will not necessarily make better engineers in the purely technical sense, but it will help engineers to enrich their own lives and the thinking of many who are not engineers.

How can an engineer get joyfully entangled in thinking about technology as a general human phenomenon? I do not know, partly because few have bothered to tell us. But there are examples. Consider the case of Herbert Hoover. As a young man in China he made a fortune in mining engineering. Then he settled in London to continue his international operations. In some way he became enchanted by early books on mining and metallurgy and began collecting them. His wife, Lou Henry Hoover, was a good Latinist, and in 1912 the two of them published in London a magnificent English version of

George Agricola's *De re metallica* of 1556. The translation was done largely by Mrs. Hoover, and the lavish geological and technical annotations were produced by Mr. Hoover. In 1913 the book reviewers of Germany were beating their breasts in humiliation that an "English" engineer and his wife had paid so great a tribute to a German classic which German scholars had neglected. The events of 1914 onward diverted the Hoovers to other matters. Cyril Stanley Smith of the Massachusetts Institute of Technology, himself a superb metallurgist, has continued this tradition to our immense profit with his annotated collaborative translations of Biringuccio, Ercker, Theophilus, and others.

As with most such dedications of the self, it seems that one simply "gets hooked" by something: there is an element of falling in love; an experience like religious conversion, however quiet. It may come so slowly that the person involved does not quite realize what is happening to him. My colleague Ladislao Reti is a case in point.

Reti was born in Fiume on the Dalmation coast when it was part of Hungary. His advanced education in engineering began in Vienna and culminated with a Ph.D. in chemistry from the University of Bologna. He emigrated to the Argentine, did some sophisticated research in chemistry, and built up a considerable chemical industry. Because of political trouble with Perón, Reti moved to São Paulo in Brazil, and there he built a second large chemical business. But by now he was buying early books in the history of science and technology, and poring over them. Gradually a trickle of articles from his pen began to appear, largely in Italian engineering journals. Several of them centered on Leonardo da Vinci.

Most students of Leonardo have been trained as humanists, are uncomfortable in the face of his massive technological interests, and have tended to stress the other aspects of his notebooks. In an effort to get a better view of Leonardo's place in the history of engineering, Reti began hunting and microfilming the many unpublished and little-known manuscripts surviving from the other technologists of the fifteenth and sixteenth centuries. He had the necessary languages; now he got the paleographic skills which this sort of document demands. He combined the methods of the humanist with the insights of the professional engineer.

The results are remarkable. Some years ago, in the Biblioteca Nazionale of Florence, I looked with some care at a notebook of the 1480s filled with engineering sketches of Buonaccorso Ghiberti, the grandson of the more famous Lorenzo Ghiberti who is best remembered for his bronze doors of the Florentine Baptistry. I found much of interest in the manuscript, but stupidly failed to understand the prize item in it. Unknown to me, Gustina Scaglia, an art historian, had recently looked at the same notebook and had recognized that some of the drawings show to us for the first time the famous derrick which Brunelleschi built in 1421 to help construct the great dome of the Cathedral in Florence. But, being only an art historian, Dr. Scaglia had no more notion than I had about just how that derrick worked. Unknown either to Scaglia or to me, Reti had already seen and identified those drawings. He had noticed that on the margin of a page containing an elaborate diagram of part of the derrick there was a small notation indicating that under the wheels illustrated there were other wheels. From his knowledge of machine design he realized at once how the apparatus worked. Returning to São Paulo, he had a model built by the tool-makers of his factory. The result is a far more sophisticated derrick than anyone had thought could be possible in the early fifteenth century.

When Reti first showed me that model, I mentioned that a few days earlier a letter from Alex Keller of the University of Leicester had said that Keller had got hints in old publications that somewhere in Madrid there were manuscripts of the Italian Giovanni Turriano, who for many years was the favorite engineer of the Emperor Charles V, and who worked largely in Spain. But Keller was feeling frustrated: he had no exact information and no funds to get to Madrid for the search. Two weeks later Reti flew to London on business, met Keller, and then flew to Madrid. There, in the Biblioteca Nacional, he found five manuscript volumes of Turriano's containing a lengthy text and hundreds of drawings recording a wide range of European technologies as they existed in the middle of the sixteenth century. Reti and Keller are now jointly preparing an edition which will amplify our knowledge greatly.

By this time Reti had decided to move from São Paulo to California to be able to use the Elmer Belt Library of Vinciana at the University of California, Los Angeles, which some consider the world's best instrument for Leonardine research. He knew that Madrid once held manuscripts of Leonardo's which more recently had fallen out of sight, and he had asked the librarians of that city to search for them. At last, early in 1967, two of them turned up, and Reti was the logical, indeed the inevitable, man to be appointed by the Spanish government to head the group of scholars responsible for editing them. One of these manuscripts is of particular interest to professional engineers, since it holds a treatise on machine design which Leonardo clearly was preparing for publication. As Reti has remarked, "At last people will start believing me when I tell them that Leonardo da Vinci was an engineer who occasionally painted a picture when he was broke."

Ladislao Reti's combination of humanistic and technological capacities may be so impressive as to discourage others from following his path. Naturally, the more one knows, the better one's work will be. But significant findings can be made even by those less well equipped.

About 1910 a French cavalry officer, Commandant Richard Lefebvre des Noëttes, retired on a pension and devoted himself for the next twenty years to his hobby, the history of harness. He came of an old military family: his grandfather had been a marshal of Napoleon's. He was not trained as a scholar, but he knew horses as no scholar had ever known them and thus could see things about them which no professional scholar had ever seen. The famous German historian of warfare, Hans Delbrück, had noted that in Antiquity cavalrymen always wielded the spear at the end of the arm, whereas in the Middle Ages they normally held the spear "at rest" under the right armpit. But Delbrück had no explanation of the change, and little sense of the great advantage in the new method. Lefebvre des Noëttes, trained as a hussar, recognized that the new style of mounted shock combat which we associate with the medieval knight was technically impossible without the stirrup; so he started out to discover when the stirrup appeared in Europe to revolutionize warfare.

Similarly, from looking at Roman pictures of horse harness he realized that it was terribly inefficient as compared with either the breast strap or the rigid collar of more recent centuries. He made some harness in the Roman style and found experimentally that the same team of horses could pull four or five times the load with modern harness that they could move with Roman. Obviously, then, the emergence of the newer harness marked an epoch in the development not only of land transport but also in the spread of horse-operated mills and hoists. The modern engineering concept of "horsepower" points to the wider significance of the new harness in the growth of Western technology. So, Lefebvre des Noëttes decided to find the origins of modern harness.

Lefebvre des Noëttes was very nearly a genius: his basic insights both remain valid and have been assimilated to the general literature of history. Unfortunately he was impetuous and failed to discipline his vast energies with the critical methods of a trained historian. He dated many of his sources wrongly, and this led him to misdate the appearance of the items he was studying, sometimes by a century or more. Therefore, he could not correlate his conclusions successfully with the wider historical movements of the early Middle Ages. One of my own adventures has been to review and expand his sources, thus making possible a more accurate dating of the appearance in Europe of the stirrup and of modern harness, both of which seem to have come from China, or at least from Central Asia. The result is a clear relation between these new means of utilizing the horse and the rapid military, social, and economic changes of the period. And the discussion continues as new evidence accumulates.

The moral of Lefebvre des Noëttes's life is that a technologist who really has a passion for the contemplation of his specialty should not be overawed by the intricate methods worked out by the guild of academic historians. He should master what he can of them; the more the better. But he should not be blocked by a sense of personal insufficiency. If his essential insights are correct and thoroughly rooted in his professional experience, his marginal errors eventually will be remedied by others. Those who rectify the blunders are usually not themselves equipped to be so magnificently mistaken.

The moral is confirmed by the last phase of Lefebvre des Noëttes's career. In his old age his interests broadened to include the whole history of medieval technology. He noticed that in Antiquity and among the Vikings the rudders of ships were lateral oars, whereas in modern times practically all vessels have vertical rudders firmly hinged to the stern post. He concluded that the stern-post rudder had many advantages, especially for oceanic voyaging, and that, indeed, the European conquest of the world after 1492 could not have been achieved with nothing better than the ancient rudder. So he attempted to date and to locate the appearance of the stern-post rudder. In a volume published in his eightieth year, he asserted that this major innovation is first found in a Northern miniature which he dated 1242. Shortly thereafter, two English scholars attempted to drive back the date by pointing to such a rudder on a relief on a baptismal font at Winchester which they dated on stylistic grounds about 1180. However, we now know that this font belongs to a family of such carvings produced at Tournai in Belgium from so hard a stone that the sculptors retained simplified forms which were a bit old-fashioned as compared with the more elaborate and naturalistic early Gothic carving which was being produced by contemporaries in softer materials. The Winchester font should be placed in the early thirteenth century, and Lefebvre des Noëttes's dating of the stern-post rudder is therefore not more than a couple of decades in error. That a landlubber French cavalryman made a major discovery in the history of the nautical arts should give us courage to do what we wish to do, provided we work hard enough at it.

In addition to a sense of historical inadequacy, there is another psychological obstacle keeping engineers from the creative contemplation of their discipline, at least in the early periods. This is the assumption that, essentially, technological advance comes from the practical application of scientific discovery. A technician will be familiar enough with the kinds of science which have influenced his specialty in his own time, but fears that he will be so out of his depth in dealing with past forms of science that he can never grasp the relations of that science to the older phases of his specialty.

The fear is groundless. Until the middle of the nineteenth century there were remarkably few connections between science and technology, and the influence of technology upon science seems to have been greater than the reverse. Science through the ages was a purely intellectual effort to comprehend nature; technology was the practical attempt to use nature for human purposes. While a few individuals, like Friar Roger Bacon or Galileo, were interested in both, they showed little interplay between their practical and their theoretical concerns. Until some four generations ago, technology was affected by theology, geography, and the like more than by science. The history of technology has been a record of inspired empiricism.

Consider, for example, the case of Thomas Newcomen's epochal atmospheric steam engine, which he built with a decade's labor between 1702 and 1712. There was, of course, an old tradition of scientific investigation of steam, vacua, and pressures. It is almost beyond belief to the modern mind that without scientific help this Devonshire ironmonger could have been the first to harness steam; yet recent and careful study shows that Newcomen was a provincial craftsman who had no contact with, or previous knowledge of, the Savery engine or the scientific work that had in fact entered into Savery's abortive machine.

The extent of Newcomen's empirical genius is indicated by his invention of the snifting valve, essential to the continuing operation of his engine. This device drew off the air which had been dissolved in the steam and which was released in the cylinder by the condensation of the steam. So far as I am aware, no scientist of Newcomen's day knew that air dissolves in water.

So great is the dominance of science in this twentieth century that empiricism has a bad name among us: it is fashionable to be a bit contemptuous of a man like Thomas Edison, who produced world-shaking results largely based on hunches rather than on equations. I would not wish to underrate the welding of theoretical science and practical technology which is typical of our time; nevertheless to assume a hierarchy of values which puts practical achievements lower than theoretical is historically not justified. The kind of pleasure which one gets from the contemplation of science is very like that which comes from philosophy, whereas the contemplation of technology is more like that of the fine arts with which engineering has traditionally been allied. Each of these latter deals with the manipulation of matter to achieve tangible and nontheoretical ends. Yet the results are capable of displaying high genius.

There is, in fact, a theoretical aspect of the history of technology which has never been explored. Let me illustrate it from the notebooks of the Italian engineers of the Renaissance.

Clack valves, plates hinged at one side, were known in Hellenistic Antiquity. As Ladislao Reti has pointed out, conical valves first appear (at least in the Western tradition) in Leonardo's notebooks, and they enter the general literature with Agostino Ramelli's famous book of machines printed at Paris in 1588. In the drawing collection of the Uffizi in Florence, I found sketches from the 1530s by the great architect and engineer Antonio da San Gallo the Younger illustrating the first spherical valves. The UCLA Library owns a unique copy of Ramelli containing a drawing and a rejected finished plate showing pumps with spherical valves which, at some expense, was re-engraved just before publication to substitute conical valves. Clearly, Ramelli thought valves were exciting. Those who know engineering better than I tell me that the clack valve is entirely satisfactory until one is dealing with liquids or gases under high pressure. The technicians of the fifteenth and sixteenth centuries were working under no such necessity; it was not until steam began to be harnessed two hundred years later that a variety of valves became essential. The great Renaissance engineers were simply taking delight in an empirical broadening of the conceptual tool chest of their profession. They were interested in finding out how many ways there are to skin a cat. Thus, when at last an authentic engineering need arose, the means of meeting it were ready.

Another set of examples may confirm the point. The technicians of the later Middle Ages and Renaissance were interested in exploring the uses of air. In the first decade of the eleventh century an Anglo-Saxon Benedictine monk named Eilmer built a glider, took off from the tower of Malmesbury Abbey, flew six hundred feet, and crashed because, as he himself said, he forgot to put "a tail on the rear end" *(caudam in posteriore parte)*. The windmill appears in 1185. Probably by the middle of the thirteenth century and certainly a bit later, rotary fans were being used to slow the fall of weights in the striking trains first of water clocks and then of mechanical clocks. The early fifteenth century shows a curious vigor in this area of technology. By 1425 the blowgun reached Italy from the Indies bringing its Malay name with it, and this stimulated work with airguns. Interest in air pressure is reflected in a Nuremberg picture of 1474 showing a wine handler using bellows to force wine through a tube from one cask to another: the earliest instance of the use of compressed air to transport materials. The suction pump, utilizing a vacuum, is first found in the 1430s in a notebook of a Sienese engineer, and in the same manuscript Reti found a child's toy, perhaps a borrowing from China, involving the helicopter principle which fascinated Leonardo at the end of the century but which did not become practical until a generation ago.

It has been generally believed that Leonardo likewise was the first to think of using air as a decelerator in the parachute. However, in the British Museum I found an unnoticed Italian manuscript which can be dated in the 1470s or the very early 1480s—that is, slightly before Leonardo's sketch of a parachute. The anonymous engineer producing this notebook first drew a picture of a man jumping and braking his fall by means of long streamers fluttering in the air and attached to his belt. In his teeth he holds a sponge to help protect his jaws from the shock of landing. He looks a bit scared, and well may be. The following eighteen pages of the manuscript show a miscellany of pumps, pile drivers, military machines, and the like. But our technician is getting worried about that fellow: he is going to break his legs. Something better must be done for him. On the nineteenth page the jumper appears again, and in much better condition. For one thing, the sponge is now held in his mouth by a strap running around his head so that he will not lose it if he cries out in terror. But more important, the fluttering streamers have been replaced by a conical parachute, the first, I believe.

Leonardo's parachute was pyramidal rather than conical; whether he saw this sketch is immaterial: the world of the engineer was full of excited communication, and the idea of the parachute, if not the thing, was in the air. The parachute finally found publication in the early seventeenth century in the famous machine book of Fausto Veranzio, a Dalmatian bishop. Thereafter it was widely known as a possibility, but no one actually jumped in one until the 1780s, three hundred years after its conceptual invention. In our own day, when the parachute is basic both to military operations and to the exploration of outer space, one may be a bit awed by the inspiration of the anonymous Italian engineer in whose fertile brain the notion of the parachute first sprouted.

Doubtless he suspected that his design of it would not really work; and indeed, it is much too small to sustain a man's weight, as were both Leonardo's and Veranzio's after him. But he was thinking on paper, groping his way. He was trying to expand the vocabulary of the engineer by inventing a new word, a new way in which mankind could relate itself to the forces and substances of the natural environment. He was bold enough not to be afraid to stammer with the novelty of what he was saying. And when, three centuries later, ballooning made parachuting functional, the concept of the parachute was ready.

The study of technology as one of the major forms of the creativity of mankind is as yet little developed. A few, like myself, who lack technical abilities and whose intellectual formation has been humanistic have been drawn to it because we found large questions about the past which seem to be unanswerable apart from technology. But our results will be very partial and subject to error until a considerable group of engineering specialists find themselves impelled to labor as passionately in the contemplation of the task to which they are devoted as they now work to accomplish concrete tasks. In discovering this hidden aspect of their existence they will find a new joy.

Under the darkening red cliffs the Navajos clustered about their fires. Suddenly the boy started talking again. "Over near Shiprock my family has a melon patch, but wolves come and eat the melons. They don't eat them right there," he said. "They take them to a place a little way off." Then a slight hesitation. "They carry them with human hands. Did you ever see a wolf who could carry a melon?" I hadn't. He said, "They are witch-wolves."

Then he began to talk even more rapidly. I was flattered that he would tell me these things. After all, he was going to a white man's school and knew that in such matters we who are called Anglos in that country are often top-lofty. I was flattered because it seemed that after two hours he knew that I wouldn't make fun of him. "My brother, the one who was killed in Korea, was out watching the sheep one night and he fell asleep. He heard a lamb cry and he woke up and against the moon he saw a great wolf with the lamb in its mouth. My brother pulled out his six-shooter and emptied it into the wolf, but the wolf paid no attention and ran off. The next day we found the lamb strung up on a tree and its head had been cut off clean with a wire. How could a wolf get a wire and do that?"

By the early 1950s things had got badly mixed up among the Navajos. Sanitary conditions had somewhat improved. Fewer babies were dying. The population was skyrocketing beyond anything which their traditional economy of sheep-herding could care for. The range was overgrazed and rapidly eroding. Officials of the Indian Service had tried to get the Navajos to cut down the size of their flocks and to improve the stock so that they could get more food and better wool from fewer sheep. Above all, the Indian Service had tried to induce the tribe to get rid of the surplus horses that devoured the range. But for generations Navajos had counted prestige in terms of the number of horses and sheep which one owns. Such suggestions ran against the grain of Navajo attitudes, and a sad history had taught them to be suspicious of advice from any white man. The result was great tension: tension with white men, but tension also between Navajos, since many of the younger ones realized that the range was being ruined and that something must be done to preserve it.

Moreover, during the Second World War thousands of Navajo men had gone out into a larger and more complex world. They had been in military service or at work in industry. Then they came back to their people, having picked up disturbing notions. For example, the family organization which is basic to the whole Navajo view of how people get on together is entirely different from the white American's. A man marries into, and usually lives with, his wife's family. A man's maternal uncles may play a larger part in his life than his father does. Such is the emphasis upon the mother's family rather than the father's. In

Navajo the words for brother and sister are also applied to the children of your mother's sisters. Property tends to be inherited through the mother's line rather than through the father's. Young Navajos going out into the American world and then returning brought back deeply subversive ideas which rent not only the fabric of Navajo society but also of Navajo emotions. They didn't know how it was proper to feel, and not knowing how it is proper to feel is even more disconcerting than not knowing how it is proper to think.

There was discord, a temper-heating friction, among the Navajos because of this pervasive uncertainty. The old foundations of right conduct, the traditional views of the universe and of man, were now doubted as they had never been doubted before. One symptom and result was a marked increase of witchcraft.

From the earliest times there have been witches. Every people has had witches or has believed in the possibility of witches. But the importance of witches seems to vary greatly according to whether a society is confident of itself or whether it is filled with self-doubt.

Innocent men and women have been persecuted for witchcraft, but it would appear from the records that many alleged witches have believed themselves in fact to be witches and have believed witchcraft to be effective. Why do people become witches? If you are feeling helpless, that something must be done about your anxieties even though there is no right solution (and if you believe likewise that demonic powers are available), then why not become a witch and utilize these powers? Government officials involved in the stock reduction program were typical targets of Navajo witchcraft.

There is, however, a more important reason why people became witches. Witchcraft is always a turning upside down of the moral standards of the world in which the witch lives. It is a drastic and spectacular way of rebelling, a repudiation of things as they are. It is an ultimate denial, a form of nihilism which is demanded by mentally and emotionally unstable people in any time of rapid change.

And why do so many people who do not themselves become witches believe so ardently in witchcraft? Because when things are going quite wrong there is an inner necessity of finding some means of explaining why they are going wrong, of explaining this rather simply, and of giving some hope that there is a remedy for the situation. As Clyde Kluckhohn, who has observed the Navajos closely, remarks, "In terms of witchcraft a person can justify his being worried without taking the blame himself . . . nothing is more intolerable to human beings than to be persistently disturbed without being able to say why or without being able to phrase the matter in such a way that some relief or control is available. Witchcraft belief allows one to talk about his anxiety in terms that are acceptable and which imply the possibility of doing something about it."

But there is another and more somber rea-

son why among the Navajos there was need for
witches and a need to believe in witchcraft. A society afflicted with self-doubt is a society torn by self-hate. It must have scapegoats. Uncertainty breeds brutality. It must find or create someone on whom to vent animosity, particularly if this hatred can't be formulated very exactly. Occasionally among the Navajos a witch was executed. According to reports, the methods were as deplorable as they always have been when witches are killed, because a social venom is excreted that way. The witch dies for the people.

There was a period in our own society when we needed witches and had them in enormous numbers. It began about the year 1300, ended somewhat after 1650, and is usually called the Renaissance. This was a time of torrential flux, of fearful doubt, marking the transition from the relative certainties of the Middle Ages to the new certainties which dominated the eighteenth and nineteenth centuries. Medieval society had been rural, agricultural, aristocratic, and essentially religious in its judgment of values. What we usually call the Modern Age — there is legitimate doubt whether we still live in it — tended to become urban, industrial, middle-class in its atmosphere, and worldly in its standards of value.

By the end of the thirteenth century the framework of the Middle Ages was beginning to crack. Everywhere the old axioms were being challenged. The greatest of medieval thinkers, St. Thomas Aquinas, died in 1274; he was scarcely buried before a philosophical revolution swept him into centuries of neglect. The new seminational monarchies were undercutting the authority of both Papacy and Holy Roman Empire. A money economy was destroying feudalism, and merchants were beginning effectively to oust aristocrats from posts of real authority. Above all, men's treasures were increasingly located in this world rather than in the next. Under such circumstances Europe had to have witches.

There were very few witches before the fourteenth century. Naturally, since witches are mentioned in the Bible, people believed in the possibility of witchcraft, and both witches and wizards, like Merlin of the Arthurian legends, appear in imaginative literature. But they were very rare in daily life. As late as the year 1258 Pope Alexander IV tells some Inquisitors to stick to their job of getting after heretics and warns them not to be sidetracked by charges of witchcraft. By 1300, however, witchcraft had been identified with heresy, and all of Europe was beginning to get excited about it.

God might rule in heaven, but it seemed more and more that Satan ruled the world. Men were becoming more interested in earthly things. How could one do better, then, than to cultivate Satan? This is the essence of the Faust Legend, the desire for power to exploit this world, and alliance with demonic forces to do it.

But even more important in the rise of Renaissance witchcraft was the motive of re-

bellion. We know from the records (and the
records of witchcraft trials often reflect an almost clinical attitude) that the urge to sorcery at times sprang from unbearable cultural tension. The Church had been the heart of the Middle Ages, and the Mass was the heart of the Church. During Mass, at the moment, say, of the elevation of the Host for the adoration of the people, someone, usually a woman, might feel an uncontrollable urge to spit or to make an obscene remark. To her unconscious mind the Host was the symbol of the whole status quo, of all the old ideas which were not coping with the new facts and the new situations. This outburst meant far more to the submerged portions of her mind than to its conscious levels. Having defied God, she felt an emancipation, an access of confidence. But this could only be diabolical. She tried it again; she got the same results. She became convinced that she was in alliance with Satanic forces; in her the worship of Satan replaced the worship of God. Thus she became, consciously and deliberately, if by delusion, a witch.

Renaissance witchcraft cannot be understood apart from the Satanic cult. The Black Mass developed shortly after 1300. In the celebration of the Catholic Mass a wafer is used with the monogram of Christ on it. The first evidence of the Black Mass turned up in 1324 with the arrest of an Irish woman among whose effects was found a wafer bearing the monogram of Satan. A few years later a French priest was arrested on charges of celebrating the

Satanic liturgy habitually. The Black Mass of the Renaissance was essentially an inversion of the Christian Mass. The Lord's Prayer was said backwards; the sign of the Cross was made with the left foot on the ground. It was schizophrenic rebellion against everything inherited by tradition. To the witches this dramatization of their nihilism gave extraordinary emotional release and a sense of power. Often they organized themselves into covens not only to celebrate their rites but to deal in drugs, potions, and poisons, and to extort what "protection" money they could from the surrounding population. That witches were deluded does not alter the fact that they were vicious.

We still know little about the human mind. No scholar as yet has had both the historical learning and the psychological insight to write an account of the social neuroses of the Renaissance. But clearly it was an age when so many people were deeply disturbed that things which we consider abnormal were raised to the level of mass phenomena and acceptance. Masochism had social sanction in the flagellants. Sadism, akin to the need to hate, led to a horrifying development of the technology of torture. Necrophilia—delight in corpses—appears in the Dance of Death, in the skeletal motifs of costume, and in the more gruesome manifestations of sepulchral art. Exhibitionism reached its culmination in the male costume of the sixteenth century.

Sporadically there would emerge mass hysterias like the St. Vitus Dance. In the 1490s,

just as the witch-hunt was approaching its
greatest excesses, epidemics of demon posses-
sion began to appear, and they remained
common well into the seventeenth century.
Communities of religious women were particularly vulnerable: there was one bizarre case
when an entire convent of nuns was possessed
and mewed and purred like cats each after-
noon.

But the greatest and most terrible manifestations of the Renaissance agony was witchcraft. Old foundations were slipping in various
measure and variously in different places, but
everywhere slipping. In the best of people and
of ages there is hatred, but out of great doubt
comes great hate. In such uncertainty some
must always find the illusion of freedom
through conspiratorial rebellion in secret
alliance with alien powers hostile to the world
they live in, while others must discover or invent an object on which to pour the bile se-
creted by their anxieties. The witch and the
witch-hunter were children of one bewilder-
ment, sharing one blind vengefulness, reflect-
ing one mentality, and stemming from one
inner necessity. In the Renaissance, as among
the Navajos, some people had to become
witches and other people had to believe in
witchcraft and to persecute witches in order to
vent the wordless turmoil within them. As an
eminent psychiatrist has said, the Renaissance
kept the witch alive in order to kill her. And
long before psychiatry was invented the wise
French historian Michelet remarked that

witches were born out of the despair of man-kind.

Their slaughter went on generation after generation. Unnumbered thousands died hideously in every part of the European world. This is one of the forgotten chapters in the history of Western civilization. But it should not be forgotten; for neurotic cruelty is not beyond the capacity of our twentieth century. In a single year a Bishop of Bamberg burned 600 witches. In Savoy 800 were condemned to death in a batch. Everyone has heard that Calvin burned Servetus as a heretic. Few know that in one year of Calvin's rule in Geneva thirty-four witches were executed. The mania crossed the Atlantic and culminated in 1692, when twenty men and women were put to death in Salem, Massachusetts, for witchcraft. In Western Europe by that time it had very nearly died out.

We do not know why about the middle of the seventeenth century, except in marginal areas like New England and Poland, it quite suddenly became unnecessary to torture and kill witches or, for that matter, heretics. The usual explanation is that at that time a new, orderly, "scientific" vision of the universe emerged, one which we usually associate with the name of Descartes but which was the product of the thinking and feeling of many men.

It has been asserted that this new cosmic sense both denied the objective possibility of witchcraft and gave Western culture such inner confidence that the venting of irrational anxiety was made obsolete. But there is an anachronism here of nearly a century: the kind of solid citizen who was responsible for witch-burning was scarcely affected, as early as 1650, by the thinking of Copernicus, Galileo, or the like, much less Descartes. The reasons for the end of the witch mania are still an enigma, as are the exact reasons for its rise at the end of the thirteenth century.

In our time we are subject not only to individual but also to group anxiety, and this seems to be related to a velocity of change which is hard to assimilate emotionally. There have been hideous episodes of irrational slaughter of scape-groups in this century. More such tragedies are inevitable unless each of us ponders more deeply the surge forward of a new culture in which we are involved as were the men of the late Middle Ages and Renaissance. Only by understanding ourselves can we tame the wolf in our hearts.

INDEX

A

Adam, Fall of, 45, 49
Adams, Ansel, viii
Adams, Henry, 57–62 *passim,* 73
Adelard of Bath, 30
Adult education, 138
Aesop, 40
Age of Faith, 68
Agricola, George, 154
Agriculture, role of, 83, 84
Agrigento, Sicily, 98
Air, uses of, 164–167
Airguns, 165
Albuquerque, 81
Alexander IV (Pope), 174
Alexandria, gunpowder artillery in, 125
al-Jazari, 117
Alphabetization, history of, 109, 110
al-Rāzī, 98, 99
Anglicans, 53
Apollinaris Sidonius, 136
Arabic scientific works, 82, 98, 124
Archimedes, 64, 115, 116
Architecture, contemporary, source of, 13
Aristocrats versus workers, 24–26, 64, 104, 141, 149
Aristotle, 15, 85, 127
Artillery, counterweight, 68
Asian influences, 14, 15, 113; *see also* China; India; Japan
Assumption of the Virgin (dogma), 53
Assyrian conquest of Jews, 35
Astronomy, and traditional Christianity, 49
Athens, first consciously Occidental society, 27
Atomic theory (atomism), 111
Ausonius, 136
Austria, cranks in, 119
Automation, 81

B

Babylonian conquest of Jews, 35
Bacon, Roger, 69, 70, 77, 89, 100, 101, 161

Baganda tribe, language of, 18
Baroque art, 103
Bellifortis (Keyser), 129
Bellows, 165
Benedictine Order, 63, 64, 104
Bessarion, on Western technology, 81
Biblioteca Nazionale, Florence, 155
Biology, and traditional Christianity, 48, 49
Biringuccio, Vannoccio, 154
Bismarck, 2
Black Mass, 175, 176
Bloch, Marc, 76
Blowgun, 165
Brunelleschi, 155
Bruno, Giordano, 46
Buddhism, 14, 52, 112
Buridan, 82
Business schools, 138
Buttons, invention of, 129, 130
Byzantium, 11, 81, 88, 121, 125

C

Caballa, Provençal, 92
Cairo, gunpowder artillery in, 126
Callinicus, 125
Calvin, John, 178
Cannons and cannon balls, 69, 122–127
Canon
  of the globe, 12, 16, 27, 31
  of the hierarchy of values, 23, 29–31
  of logic and language, 15, 16, 28, 31
  of the Occident, 11–13, 16, 27, 31
  of rationality, 20, 29, 31
  of the spectrum of values, 23, 25, 29–31
  of symbols, 16–18, 28, 31
  of the unconscious, 20–23, 29, 31
Canons of culture, changing, 11–31
Cartesianism; *see* Descartes
Cathar heresy, 92, 101, 102